Paths of Faithfulness

Personal Essays on Jewish Spirituality

Edited by

Carol Ochs,
Kerry M. Olitzky,
and
Joshua Saltzman

KTAV Publishing House, Inc.
1997

Library of Congress Cataloging-in-Publication Data

Paths of faithfulness : personal essays on Jewish spirituality / edited by Carol
Ochs, Kerry M. Olitzky, and Joshua Saltzman.
     p.   cm.
     Includes bibliographical references.
     ISBN 0–88125–596-3 (alk. paper)
     1. Spiritual life—Judaism. 2. Jewish way of life. 3. Hebrew Union
College–Jewish Institute of Religion. New York School— Faculty—
Religious Life. I. Ochs, Carol. II. Olitzky, Kerry M. III. Saltzman, Joshua.
     BM723.P37   1997
     296.7—dc21   97–5078
                                                       CIP

Publication is made possible, in part, by The Nathan Cummings Foundation

Manufactured in the United States of America
KTAV Publishing House, 900 Jefferson Street, Hoboken NJ, 07030

Rabbi Baer once said to his teacher, the Seer of Lublin, "Show me one general way to the service of God." The Tzaddik replied: "It is impossible to tell a person what way to take. For one way to serve God is through learning, another through prayer, another through fasting, and still another through eating. We should carefully observe what way our heart draws us to, and then choose this way with all our strength."

Contents

Introduction

The recognition and celebration of diverse paths to serve God is one of the great strengths of Reform Judaism, as it offers every Jew a chance to worship with authenticity and wholeness. This openness is most apparent in the thoughtful and deeply personal searching of the faculty of the Hebrew Union College–Jewish Institute of Religion in New York. Asked to reflect on the ways they live out their own calls to holiness, the faculty have contributed a collection of widely diverse essays explaining their individual paths, each of which takes them to a lifelong commitment to *kedushah* (holiness). For one it is the path of study, for another a path of action, for a third a path of personal relationship, for a fourth a mystic way. Each path includes elements of the other ways. What makes these ways uniquely

Reform is the emphasis placed on holiness and the significance assigned to personal responsibility for shaping and discerning the way. Each one puts together a way built on the three pillars of the tradition: Torah, God, and People. And each of these foci is further enriched by many layers of meaning and association. Torah is binding law and also water that refreshes us in the desert of our ordinary lives; God is the source of all holiness and also an intimate friend; People represents Jewish tradition and history, and also family and ethics. A proposed fourth pillar, Land, is a political response to antisemitism and represents the sacredness of place.

The contributors bring to this volume a broad cross-section of backgrounds, experience, and views. They include women as well as men, younger scholars as well as those long established, rabbis and laypersons. All of them together show the richness of the Reform vision, a vision that celebrates diversity, individual responsibility, and an unending quest for the holy. These are the paths of faithfulness that the faculty of the New York School have chosen. They invite their students to develop their own paths out of love for Torah, God, People, and Land, configured to their unique gifts.

About the Essays

Sherry H. Blumberg: "Jewish Spirituality: Toward My Own Definition" increases the number of spiritual paths to include such paths as: loyalty, relationship, curiosity and genuine dialogue, passion, joy, justice, compassion, self-reflection, creativity, balance and wholeness.

Eugene B. Borowitz: "My Father's Spirituality and Mine" explores four forms of living Jewishly, the committed actions of his socially concerned father, the study of his grandfather, the spirituality embodied by one of his teachers, and the mystic way that he admires but does not emulate.

Michael Chernick: "Ki Hashem Elokekha Esh Okhlah: Spirituality and Danger" defines spirituality as living one's life knowing that you are in the presence of God.

Martin A. Cohen: "What is Jewish Spirituality?" presents the historical context for the term spirituality and sees Torah as our unique way.

Norman J. Cohen: "*Etz Ḥayyim Hi:* It is a Tree of Life" finds Torah study to be that which most consistently brings him to a sense of God's presence.

A. Stanley Dreyfus: "Random Observation on Spirituality" finds his spiritual fulfillment in a classical Reform worship service and study of Hebrew texts.

Lawrence A. Hoffman: "Reform Religious Zionism: Celebrating the Sacred in Time and Space" extends the traditional three bases of Judaism: people, God, and Torah to include a fourth focus, land—in the metaphysical sense of sacred space analogous to the diaspora's regular experience of sacred time.

Lawrence S. Kushner: "This is Your Life: Reflections on Jewish Spirituality" uses brief incidents in his life to help us sense the ongoing mystery and wonder.

Philip E. Miller: "Some Personal Thoughts on Jewish Spirituality" is an ongoing development which forms the nexus of his everyday religious life.

Carol Ochs: "Jewish Spirituality: The Way of Love" focuses on how all the paths take on an inner reality through love.

Kerry M. Olitzky: "Toward a Personal Definition of Jewish Spirituality" gives new meaning to study, prayer, and *mitzvot* as he shows what these terms have come to mean in his own life.

Lawrence W. Raphael: "My Spiritual Journey" makes all the speculation deeply personal when he shares the ethical will he wrote for his children.

Joshua Saltzman: "Talmud Torah and Spirituality: A Postmodern Perspective" takes a postmodern approach to Jewish life tempered by the deeply experienced encounter with a teacher.

Nancy Wiener: Hineni—Ehyeh Asher Ehyeh emphasizes the ways in which we are in the image of God: by aspiring to wholeness, integrity, and the ongoing process of becoming.

My Father's Spirituality and Mine

Eugene B. Borowitz

My father was as good a Jew and human being as I have ever met. Yet I wonder if people in this generation would consider him "spiritual." (I think they would respond more immediately to my mother's "spirituality," but, because it was so primally entwined with her fineness of soul, it would take more poetic skill than I have to describe it.) He and my mother attended Friday night services with great regularity, and late Saturday afternoons my dad would often take me, as a young teenager, to the temple's *shaleh-shudas* (= *shalosh se'udah*), where he was often one of the youngest people present (a smallish number to begin with). I vaguely recall that his davening on these occasions seemed more perfunctory than intense. Though he enjoyed having certain rituals performed, he always managed to find

1

ways to have more "learned" people conduct them, e.g., our
Seders. Thus, I do not recall his ever having made *Kiddush*.
His "study" consisted of a thoughtful perusal of the daily
Forverts (which, in Columbus, Ohio, the mailman delivered). He esteemed learning and the educated, so my sister
was long the only female college-graduate in our extended
family, and the academic expectations of me were lovingly
high.

His outstanding Jewish virtue, after devotion to our family, was his love of Jews, an attitude he then also applied to
everyone else in the world. When as a young man he read
in the Communist daily, *Freiheit,* that the Jewish settlers in
Palestine were exploitative colonialists who had provoked
the Arab riots of the late 1920s, he threw the paper in the
garbage and became a reader of the Socialist *Forverts.* He
represented the Jewish Labor Committee to the Columbus
Jewish Community Council (though he managed production
in a large trouser factory), and I remember sitting outside
the room of one hot Council session waiting for him when
the issues of refugees and Zionism were boiling. He was
aroused and told the Council that he could not say what he
needed to say in his English (ordinarily quite workable), so
he asked for the right to address the Council in Yiddish, the
only time that ever happened in that German-American-
dominated august body. (I could only hear muffled sounds
coming from the room, but I could tell that he had been
most passionate.) During World War II he was instrumental
in racially integrating the production lines in his factory, the

first time that happened at an industrial plant in Columbus. (And only the Jewish admonitions of clean speech keep me from repeating the line with which he spurned those workers who wanted segregated bathrooms.)

In the 1960s with their death-of-God agitation, I once asked my father if he believed in God. He looked at me as if that were a peculiar question to ask and said, "Of course," as if no sensible person would do otherwise. That was that. When, some years later, he was dying of pancreatic cancer, fortunately without intractable pain, and I was walking with him in Sloan-Kettering Memorial Hospital, he quietly said to me at one point, "*Ich hob mein's getun,*" "I did mine." That was as much of a summing up as he needed, as much of a statement of purpose and duty as I ever heard from him. The rest was all good-hearted deed.

By today's preferred understanding of "spirituality," I doubt that my father would qualify as a model. He certainly wasn't very self-conscious about God or his relationship to God, nor did he judge his acts by whether they made God more present in his life or that of society. People now use "spirituality" to refer to a religiosity which is more interior, more subjective, more explicitly God-oriented than my father's. I never heard him use that term or anything like it to speak of others and certainly not about himself. He probably would have shaken his head in incomprehension at it, considering it another of those American things that others found valuable but he didn't understand or value.

The gap between my father's living Jewishness and our concern about Jewish spirituality set me to thinking. If, by the American Jewish standards of his time, my father was a good Jew without our kind of spirituality, what might I learn about our sense of Jewish piety by thinking about him and some other fine Jews I have known?

Over the years I have often been reminded of my father's dedication when talking to one or another rabbinic colleague, generally not people on the national scene or of great reputation. When they talked about their work, I was moved by their simple devotion to it, the unending round of services, hospitals, simchas, committee meetings, community affairs, and more. They also complained a good deal, particularly about the heavy workload. I was, after all, a rare safe, sympathetic ear, one unlike their spouses, who they felt might already be suffering from an overload of their kvetching. Yet once the ventilation was over, what remained was their quiet determination to carry on with their rabbinic tasks as best they could. They knew that this was what they most wanted, most needed to do. God bless them, they sent me away from such encounters renewed in shouldering my own kind of rabbi-burdens, convinced that there were more good Jews in the rabbinate than our critical community—myself included—ever appreciated.

I now think of these colleagues and my father as exemplars of a classic type of Jewish spirituality. In their different ways they followed the rabbinic ideal of the *tzaddik,* the Jew whose good deeds win God's approval. Most contemporary Jews, I guess, will more readily identify this type of activist Jewishness with people who have devoted their lives to great ethical issues. That was surely my sense of some of the (apparently secularistic) colleagues who put themselves on the line in the early days of the civil rights struggle and who have tried to carry on the good fight in less dramatic ways ever since. But where the *tzaddik*-hood of ethical devotion has often been celebrated in our movement, its more ordinary, everyday elaboration deserves greater attention.

In some ways my father's activist Judaism accords poorly with his childhood, for it was tied up with another ideal Jewish type. My father grew up in the home of his maternal grandfather, awaiting for over a decade his American immigrant father's call to his wife and children in Poland to join him. Of Hershel, his grandfather, of whom my father always spoke with reverence, he particularly remembered how he stopped being the *rav* of Sokoly and instead, since he had the special *semihah* allowing him to grant others *semihah,* turned his house into a modest yeshiva over which he then presided. He was, apparently, a Jew in the classic Litvak mode, one whose spirituality took the form of study and the intellectual exercise that accompanied it. I no longer remember whether he was a *musmakh* of Volozhin or Slobodka (as I once wrote), but it was clear he was a *mitnagged* who observed the ban on Hasidism. So he was undoubtedly influenced by the classic text of Litvak spirituality, the *Nefesh ha-Hayyim* of Hayyim Volozhiner (the Vilna Gaon's disciple and the Volozhin *rosh yeshivah*). That work identifies Torah with the *Ein-Sof,* making study the Litvak equivalent of the *unio mystica* some Jews today take to be the goal of spirituality. Being a *masmid,* an unceasing student of Torah, was for such Jews a way to literally be in God's presence. Despite his love for Hershel, my father did not have the *sitzfleisch* to become a *ḥakham* and, though he urged education upon me, he made it clear that he thought intellect without deeds a betrayal of Jewish responsibility.

Perhaps the purest Litvak-style intellect I ever came across was my teacher Samuel Atlas. He was an acknowledged master in both philosophy and Talmud, the two disciplines he taught at Hebrew Union College. It remains one of the great regrets of my life that his understanding was so advanced and mine so rudimentary that I could not benefit from his utterly uncommon interdisciplinary mastery. Some of my other teachers, themselves dauntingly learned, also exemplified the Jewish piety of determined intellectuality. Julian Morgenstern, a leading Semitic linguist and biblical scholar of his day; Samuel Cohon, who taught theology from what seemed like an encyclopedic knowledge of Judaism; and Sheldon Blank, who meticulously attended to the words of the prophets and gently made them the standard of his life—they were all people who realized themselves most fully in the exercise of the mind. These scholars considered their subjective lives a private matter, yet their piety in and through their intellectuality was evident to anyone sensitive. *Mutatis mutandis,* they were not what the rabbis meant by *ḥakhamim* nor my great-grandfather's kind of Litvak, yet a single kind of Jewish religiosity linked them—and, if I may say so, is what animates the instruction at our New York School. That I followed Hershel's way was no rebellion against my father. He not only encouraged me in it but kept me a lifetime doer as well as thinker.

The more personalistic, felt piety that we today largely identify with Jewish spirituality was not without its exemplars years ago, though it was no one's spoken goal. To stay with rabbis—though some marvelous lay examples could easily be adduced—let me say a few words about a somewhat older colleague, Byron T. Rubenstein. "B.T.," as everyone called him, always seemed an unusual spirit. It's hard to know why people universally felt that way about him but perhaps it indicates that we all have a certain openness to genuine piety even if we insist it is not our own way to live. B.T.'s aura of spirituality didn't have anything to do with what he said about himself or directly urged on others. On the surface he seemed like most other good rabbis. And it didn't keep him from the life of deeds—he was the oldest rabbi (forty-something, I would guess) among the sixteen of us (and Al Vorspan) who answered Martin Luther King's telegram to a CCAR convention inviting us to come get arrested in his campaign in St. Augustine, Florida. Yet you knew he was a person of great inner depth, an unusually elegant spirit, someone whose simple wholeheartedness you would like to emulate if you ever could.

Our present discussion of spirituality has, I think, gone somewhat further on B.T.'s road by making interiority a value to be sought consciously, by struggling with how to give it adequate verbal expression, and by identifying it unambiguously with personal experience of God. These are not small gains, for in our time the subjective side of religion has not been given its due, so we are engaged in an effort to add the Judaism of the heart to that of the deed and the mind. We are learning to value not only the *tzaddik* and the *ḥakham* but the psalmist as well.

Some have gone even further and seek the path of the kabbalist. Zalman Schachter-Shalomi, Art Green, and Larry Kushner, each in his own way, set before us models of contemporary Jewish mystic spirituality. Within limits, I can appreciate their form of Jewish spirituality. I say that because, though I admire how mystic experience has affected them and their teaching, I have not shared their experience of merger with the Divine. Like Buber, I find the apparent fulfillment of the self becoming one with the Ultimate less significant than standing on my own side of the I-Thou hyphen, marvelously involved, yet respectful of the Other's individuality—and my own.

So I have known four kinds of Jewish spirituality in my lifetime, ones amply attested in Jewish tradition. What gives me pause in my otherwise wholehearted appreciation of the new personalistic emphasis among us is what often troubled me about one or another form of Jewish piety in the past, that emphasizing one aspect of Jewishness, they will not give proper scope to the others. At the moment, I do not see much danger that the new interiority will decrease our concern with ethics and rite. The psalmist is no stranger to the needed deed. But there is a certain American anti-intellectualism which easily co-opts subjectivity to deny or constrict the role that learning and thinking play in the service of God. Not everyone is gifted to be a *ḥakham*. Most of us would be happy to qualify as their disciples, *talmidei ḥakhamim*. What concerns me only is properly holistic spirituality, one in which, depending on temperament and opportunity, we do not turn our backs on either the doer, the student, or the believer in us, but find our way to give them a dynamic unity in our lives.

Jewish Spirituality: Toward My Own Definition

Sherry H. Blumberg

For most of my life I have been trying to get people to talk about, think about, and teach about God. It seems to me that talking about, struggling with, challenging, loving, drawing near, and cleaving to God is the core of Jewish spirituality.

Often I have used the word "spiritual" or "religious" when arguing that we need to talk about God to express our Jewish spirituality. To be religiously Jewish instead of just culturally or ethnically Jewish is important to me, and I think important for this generation.

As I moved from the practical world of the religious school into the more academically oriented world of Hebrew Union College–Jewish Institute of Religion, I found the need to develop clearer definitions of my words. For a while I found Neal Gillman's definition to be satisfactory.

11

. . . let us define spirituality then as that which, according to the believer, God demands above all. God demands many things, forms of behavior, emotions, a set of beliefs, or intellectual formulations . . . by spirituality, we are trying to get at that form of religious expression which the believer considers indispensable. It is the ultimate focus of his religious energy, that dimension on which he places supreme emphasis. It defines the authentic believer at his best.

Gillman's definition allowed for the normative Jewish paths to God: meeting God in worship/prayer, finding God in study, and finding and serving God by doing *mitzvot* (*tzedakah, gemilut ḥasadim,* and the ritual *mitzvot*). Gillman's definition reflected Heschel's definitions of religious experience that I explored in my doctoral dissertation.

But soon I found that Gillman's definition went only one way—from God to us. What God demands is important, but I wanted a definition that also went from us to God. I wanted a relationship, an experience of God or godliness that enriches us because we are doing that which God demands. As "chutzpadik" as it may sound, I wanted to feel that beyond the continuation of the Jewish people, I personally was receiving nourishment from the covenantal relationship into which I had entered. Admittedly, this felt almost selfish, as if I should be able to love God unconditionally in the same way that I love my child.

And so I began to struggle with my definition of Jewish spirituality in the same way that I had struggled with my conceptions of and experiences with God. While I still place what God demands of me and of us as a people first, I have come to understand that I also have to make demands of my relationship with God. Sometimes what is expected of me leads to a feeling of wholeness, of deep gratitude for the miracles of life, and of great love. But I have learned that if I do not ask of God, then I cannot possibly receive. If what I ask for is the ability to serve God and others with a whole heart, to use my own gifts to their fullest advantage, and to find in each person and each moment the holiness present therein, then God responds. If I ask for strength to endure pain and suffering, to find purpose in even the worst of things, then God is present and the love that I have given is returned in full.

When asked now what Jewish spirituality means to me, I call to mind several texts: "God is in this place and I did not know" (Gen. 28:16); "I am Joseph your brother, is my father yet alive?" (Gen. 45:3); "Sing unto God a new song" (Ps. 149:1).

The first conveys the idea that God is present everywhere and we are not always aware of God's presence. That God's world is filled with wonder and beauty, and we are its caretakers, the ones who bear the responsibility to find God's presence in all things, is for me a challenge that I find in this verse.

The second reminds me that we must be aware and caring of our "brothers"—all the human beings and animals who share this planet with us—and that we must confront each other as brothers, connecting ourselves to the common heritage of our Father. We must learn to answer Cain's question "Am I my brother's keeper?" with a resounding yes.

The third verse teaches that each of us must learn to sing a new song—our own song to God. As each of us is unique, each of us will sing a different song. Whatever song we sing, we must be wholehearted with God.

When asked now to define Jewish spirituality, I find that I have broadened my definition to include not only what God requires of us, but also how we serve God as we express ourselves in our everyday lives. Thus, as a scholar in residence, I have spoken about the alternative paths to Jewish spirituality. We can serve God if we are conscious of serving by turning our own special paths into ways of service.

I have defined the alternative paths as the Path of Loyalty to Jewish people, to Israel, to family, and to friends; the Path of Relationships, developing the I-Thou relationship and truly caring when we teach, marry, parent; the Path of Curiosity and Genuine Dialogue, which leads to understanding and discoveries that make life better; the Path of Passion, which elevates and leads to the creation of special gifts to the person and others who can share in the passions; the Path of Joy and Laughter, for it says in Midrash Rabbah to Psalm 24, "Serve God in joy"; the Path of Justice combined with the Path of Compassion and Mercy, which has given us people who fight for causes that demand we think and care for this world; the Path of Self-Reflection, Self-Consciousness, and Self-Control with the Path of Self-Transcendence in which meditation, prayer, and thoughtful evaluation of self lead one closer to God and others; the Path of Creativity in all areas (arts, science, business, teaching, etc.), which enriches not only the creator but also those who share in the benefits of the creation, this also is a path of beauty; and the Path of Balance and Wholeness in everyday life. While some of these paths overlap, each of them provides a way to meet and serve God while using the talents and gifts that one has as an individual. Our responsibility is to use the talents that lead us on these paths to the best and fullest of our capacities in ethical ways that serve God and the people of Israel as we actualize ourselves. These paths then become "spiritual paths" in which God and we are partners.

In sum, I believe that our definitions of Jewish spirituality grow and change as does our relationship with God. I am excited about where my definition is now, especially when I reflect on where it has grown from. Yet I am also amazed that I can still say that talking about, struggling with, challenging, loving, drawing near, and cleaving to God is the core of my Jewish spirituality.

I am also deeply grateful and humbled by the fact that by asking of God, I have received far more than I ever dreamed, and that by responding to what God demands, I have felt a sense of purposefulness that enriches my everyday life. When I reflect upon God's presence in all of the earth, when I open my arms to my "brothers" as did Joseph, and when I sing my own new song to God as joyously as I can, then I am filled with love and wonder and hope.

Ki Hashem Elokekha Esh Okhlah: Spirituality and Danger

Michael Chernick

I have often defined spirituality as "living one's life know-ing that one is in the presence of God." That definition is exactly formulated in order to distance Jewish spirituality from two alternative spiritual possibilities: *unio mystico* spir-ituality and "warm fuzzies" spirituality. I seek to distance Jewish spirituality from these other religious experiences—and they are religious experiences—because I perceive them to be dangerous to Jews who indulge in them and to the Jewish enterprise in general.

The statement I have made raises the question of what I consider the Jewish enterprise and how I define the two spiritualities I have mentioned. Regarding the first, I believe that Judaism asks at least three things of its religiously com-mitted adherents: (1) an acknowledgment of God's exist-

17

ence and uniqueness; (2) an acceptance of the idea that the
Jewish people and God have covenanted with each other;
and (3) an agreement that the Jewish people and all its individual constituent members fulfill their part of the covenant
by active response to God's covenantal demands. Fulfillment of covenant responsibilities allows the Jewish people
to, at least, call upon God to fulfill the promises made to the
Jewish people as part of the covenantal agreement. This last
point is not, however, a requirement of Judaism. It is, rather,
an option that the Jewish people may, at its discretion,
make use of.

The purpose of the covenant is to make the Jewish people into an *am segulah,* a distinct people, with a world-task
to accomplish. That task is to function as the repository of
the highest ethical and spiritual visions possible and to
develop active means to carry out those visions. Fulfillment
of this task is carried out so that the world community may,
at its discretion, borrow from the Jewish community's vision
just as the Jewish community affirms external communities'
ethical and spiritual perceptions when it borrows higher
norms from them.[1]

The Dangers of *Unio Mystico* Spirituality

This lays the groundwork for my concerns about the two
spiritualities I referred to above. *Unio mystico,* "mystical
union with God," may not be impossible from a Jewish perspective, but I would caution against attempting it. The

---

1. BT *Hullin* 33a and Tosafot *ad hoc.*

attempt to be "one with God" is self-annihilating, and, there-fore, a form of suicide. It is this thirsting for unity with the Beloved that generated my title. One needs to remember that "the Eternal . . . is a consuming fire." The search for a constant sense of oneness with the Creator is so emotionally draining that it finally wears out the devotee both physically and mentally.

Some of the best-known victims of this passion were Menaḥem Mendel of Kotsk and the Bratslaver. The first spent practically the last twenty years of his life under his own lock-and-key. He spoke only to the first Gerer Rebbe during that time, and to no one else. He appears to have had the equivalent of a nervous breakdown, the result, if I may interpret his situation, of his heartbreaking and unending attempt to become one with God's perfection and truth.

The Bratslaver died in his thirties. I would ascribe his death to overexertion. Between trying to maintain a con-stant state of *devekut* and, at the same time, restoring the purity of *ḥasidut,* the man immolated himself in the *esh okhlah*.

Both of these Hasidic masters left tremendous spiritual legacies, but consider the price they paid. Therefore, I would not recommend their *unio* experiences to anyone. I believe that traditional Judaism has apportioned "Otherness" to God, and "being God's image (but not God's self)" to us. This suggests that, while *unio* may be available, it was never regarded as a first-rate Jewish desideratum.

The Fraudulence of "Warm Fuzzies Spirituality"

I must say, however, that *unio* ranks as the most worthwhile of Jewish spiritual pursuits when compared with what I call "warm fuzzies" spirituality. I have purposely chosen a derogatory name for this variety of spirituality because I regard it as Jewishly fraudulent and inane. It is the feeling of being loved and cared for by God, who is always good and kind and sweet-natured. This "God" always seems to be present in "caring communities" where there is lots of singing, hugging, crying, and "openness."

But one must ask, Does one experience God or community in this form of "spirituality"? Probably the latter. But God is God, and community is community; they are not the same. Indeed, the sadness of *fin de siècle* loneliness and neediness is vividly clear when any somewhat decent experience of community can be viewed as an epiphany. Further, this "spirituality" is rather narcissistic. It depends on the pleasure it gives the everpresent and everdemanding "me." Thus God is reduced to a source of personal pleasure, and as soon as the going gets rough, the "devotee" abandons the "service of God" since it only existed to serve the self.

Further, warm fuzzies spirituality demands nothing in the way of action, knowledge, or struggle with issues of faith. Instead, it finds satisfaction in the trappings and appearances of religiosity that also contribute to feeding the narcissistic self. "What a saint so-and-so is! Look how s/he prays (observes, preaches, etc.)!" From a Jewish perspective, the fraudulence of this "spirituality" is its lack of virtue and virtuosity, both absolute requirements of traditional Judaism, its lack of true worship of *Adonai Yitbarakh Shemo,* and its lack of active living out of commitments to the *Borei Olam*'s world.

Toward an Authentic Jewish Spirituality

Having warned the spiritual seeker away from *unio* and warm fuzzies, what am I proposing as an honest Jewish spirituality?

I would suggest that authentic Jewish spirituality has three components: (1) recognizing that one is living in God's presence; (2) studying God's Torah in a personally engaged fashion; and (3) acting out of these experiences in God's world. All three components join to become what in traditional parlance is called *avodat Hashem.* Note, the focus of spiritual intention here is not on self-annihilation in God or the use of God for personal satisfaction. Rather, one commits to serving God in all of one's actions by keeping as focused as possible on the question, What does God want of me (us) in this situation? God's actual Otherness is thus preserved, while we, as human beings, remain distinctly, and dignifiedly, ourselves in relation to God.

Avodat Hashem is not mere service, though service is a component of it. Ultimately, *avodat Hashem* is the recognition that one is *eved Hashem,* God's slave, no less than God's servant. Let me first deal with service, which is certainly the easier piece of Jewish spirituality than the God's-slave aspect.

Service legitimately allows us to arrive at personal and communal answers to the key question whose answer generates what God wants of me (us) in this situation. In many instances we have information regarding that question. The information appears in Torah, God's general directives for service. Here I would stress "general directives" as the operative phrase. There is no greater sign of God's love and respect for our humanness than the general formulation of God's mitzvot. This allows us to be privy to God's concerns without being totally dominated. Thus, with the generalities of the mitzvah system as a guide, we proceed to create the ways and means for its observance.[2]

In the preceding paragraph I noted that in many instances we have information about God's will. Nevertheless, there are *mitzvot kelaliyot* (general) that require us to recognize that God's will transcends specific situational mitzvot. These demand that we act on the basis of our sense of what God would desire in situations where there is no specific directive in God's Torah. Therefore, for example, it is we who must figure out what we need to do in order to fulfill the general demand of *kedoshim tihyu*. Similarly, it is an expectation of Judaism that different people will have different ideas about how to observe the obligation of "doing the just and good in God's sight" (Deut. 6:18).[3]

---

2. See Deut. 17:8–11. The passage indicates that, in most cases, all decisions regarding the specifics of any *mitzvah*'s observance are left in human hands. See also BT *Bava Metzia* 89a–b.

3. See Ramban, *Commentary on the Torah,* Lev. 19:1, s.v. *kedoshim,* and Maggid Mishneh, *Mishneh Torah,* Laws of Neighbors 14:8.

All this constitutes a service of God which includes taking God's presence seriously, contemplating the Torah's demands in an engaged, personal way, and constructing a program for realizing in the "real world" the commitments deriving from these activities. But what of "God's slavery"?

Again, let us define our terms. I mean by the term *avodat Hashem* one who recognizes himself or herself as God's slave, that is, one who is prepared to submit to God's will when such submission is demanded. Fortunately, this does not happen often, but when it does, the one from whom such submission is sought usually experiences a crisis. When the crisis is minor, usually only the intellect rebels. When the crisis is major, the entire personality of the believer goes into upheaval. It is in this furnace that spiritual commitment is tested, made, or broken.

God asks us to be a slave in those instances in which we are asked by God to inflict unjust pain on others or endure it ourselves. Something as commonplace as a *berit milah* falls into this category. There is no need for it that can be justified by the mind. It is foisted upon someone who has no choice in the matter, and who, knowing what we know of Jewish history, might prefer not to be marked in such a way. Nevertheless, though the mind rebels and the heart accedes to the rebellion, we are called upon to circumcise our males as part of our covenantal responsibility. For reasons not always quite fathomable, most of us submit and choose this for our boys. But would we choose to deny them marriage to a *mumzeret?*

The worst of spiritual and religious crises is that of human pain. This may be experienced in our own physical or emotional anguish or in the suffering of others, close or distant to us. Frequently enough this pain is not proportional to our sins, whatever they may be, and therefore such anguish weakens, if it does not obliterate, our faith in a just and loving God. Once this faith is damaged, religious spirituality that depends on one's living in God's presence is also attenuated, sometimes to the breaking point. Here, again, is a moment in which we are asked to be God's submissive slaves, *le-kabel yesurim be-ahavah,* to accept God's chastisement lovingly. How many of us could really do that if called upon to?

If you do not know the answer to that question, be patient. You will have to face the question eventually, since no human life passes without experiencing, if not witnessing, its own often painful end. That alone should make each one of us rebel. Yet most of us do not. If we do not, is it because we have submitted to God and are grateful for the time allotted us? Or have we just accepted the inevitable? Or are we simply in denial for most of our lives? How this question is answered colors the totality of one's life as a spiritual person. But if one can suffer and yet believe, though the belief is expressed in anger, and sometimes even rage, at God, one has experienced religious spirituality at its most challenged and challenging level. For all that, it remains against the letter and spirit of Jewish tradition to wish for such a challenge. I, for one, pray that God may spare me and you such challenges for as long as possible.

I do not know how many of us are ready to become the

total devotees that slavery to God demands. Still, the tradition tells us that no one is truly free save the one who has accepted the yoke of heaven upon his or her shoulders. May our spiritual searches lead us to comprehend this mystery of freedom-born-of-submission, but let us not indulge in subservience beyond the measure absolutely required by the Master of our lives. Here the words of the traditional *Siddur* may be our best guide to balance:

> *Mah namar lifanekha Hashem Eloheinu ve-Elohei Avoteinu? Ha-lo kol ha-geborim kein lefanekha, ve-anshei ke-lo hayu, ve-ḥakhamin k'beli hayu, ve-ḥakhamin k'beli madah, va-nevonim k'bli ha-sekhel? Ki rov ma'aseihem teheiyu, ve-yamei ḥeihem hevel lefanekha, ve-mutar ha-adam min ha-beheimah ein, ki ha-kol hevel.*
>
> *Aval anakhnu amekha, benei beritkha, benei Avraham ohavekha . . .*

What can we say before You, our God and God of our ancestors? Are not all the mighty like nothing before You, and the renowned as if they had never existed, and the wise as if lacking in all knowledge, and the understanding as if without sense? For all their deeds are empty, and their lives mere vanity, and the superiority of man over the beast is nonexistent, for everything is vapid.

But, nevertheless, we are Your people, the children of Your covenant, the descendants of Abraham, Your lover. . . .

Indeed, we are. And, therefore, we have the right to our spiritual patrimony in all its richness, difficulty, challenge, and depth. *Bo'u ve-rashua*! Come, claim what is yours!

What is Jewish Spirituality?

Martin A. Cohen

A s it is generally employed in the Western world, the term "spirituality" derives from classical Christianity. Classical Christianity distinguishes between spirit and matter, and therefore derivatively between spirituality and materiality. In this dualism, influenced by Plato, spirituality connotes the supernatural and the religious, while materiality refers to the natural order and the secular world. The spiritual is regarded as the domain of the good, while the material is the residence of evil. On the human plane, the material is coextensive with the corporeal, while the spiritual comprehends the noncorporeality of mind and emotion. In this polarized worldview, the logically ultimate ideal is to transcend all materiality and to live life on the spiritual plane.

The term "spirituality" is foreign to many other religions,

as well as to other applied philosophies to which the appellation of religion is not ordinarily given. Yet, in unmistakable correspondence with Christian spirituality, it is the earnest quest in all of these systems for a connection to life's meaning and purpose beyond its basal existence. If the term "spirituality" is foreign to them it is because they possess different worldviews; that is, they possess different fundamental perspectives on life. Within the diverse worldviews of these applied philosophies, the concerns of the spirit as we articulate them are couched in terms radically different from ours.

With this in mind, spirituality may inclusively be regarded as the sum of the efforts of the human psyche, individually and collectively, to attune to the impulses and rhythms of the universe, whether internal to the individual or external in nature. If realized, this attunement produces a sense of participation in the goodness and beauty of existence and connection to the awe and sanctity of life. It raises living to a plane of loftiness, perhaps even of proleptic eternity, that transcends the constrictions of our quotidian existence.

During the Middle Ages Judaism generated a concept of spirituality akin to that of Christianity. The concept is embodied in the Hebrew term *ruḥaniyut* (sometimes *ruḥanut*). The word *ruḥaniyut* is derived from *ru'aḥ,* meaning "wind" and derivatively "spirit."

References to *ruḥaniyut* spirituality reappear in the modern Jewish world. As in the medieval world, these references attest to the increased communication by Jews with our surrounding societies and the influence upon us of their thought. The current interest in spirituality by Jews derives from the parallel and even prior interest in spirituality by non-Jews in our society. This explains why the current expression of spirituality by Jews reflects the worldview of our surrounding society rather than that of the Judaism of the ages.

Yet, despite its frequency in medieval and modern Jewish life, *ruḥaniyut* spirituality is only tangential to the Jewish faith. In all cases it represents an assimilationist position in Jewish life which has at no time informed more than a small minority of the Jewish community.

Especially inconsistent with the operational worldview of centrist Judaism through the ages has been the dichotomy between spirit and matter. In the mainstream of the sacred tradition of Judaism, a wholly different division exists: it is the division between the sacred and the profane. Unlike spirit and matter, the dichotomy between the sacred and the profane is relative, not absolute. In Judaism the goal of human life is not to depreciate the material in favor of the spiritual, but rather to elevate all that is profane to the realm of the sacred. This means, in effect, that truly Jewish spirituality involves not a rejection of material existence, nor a flight from it. Rather it entails a passionate and sanctifying engagement with the totality of life.

And the means toward this sanctification, representing the distinctively Jewish understanding of spirituality, is and has always been what the tradition of Judaism calls Torah. As is well known, the concept of Torah is of supreme importance in Judaism. It is no anomaly that the word

"Torah" arguably appears more frequently in the sacred literature of our faith than any other theological concept, except for God, whose word the Torah embodies and thereby serves as a link with Divinity.

The word "Torah" in Judaism best defines not only our distinctive spirituality, but our distinctive understanding of faith. We can best express the nature of Judaism by saying that Judaism is the religion of Torah. In fact, just as the term "Israel" best defines our historic faith-people, "Torah" is the best way to designate our faith, especially once we realize that the term "Judaism" has been externally imposed and is not used in our sacred literature as our faith designation.

For some, the word "Torah" may require a brief explanation. The word "Torah" without the definite article is to be distinguished from "The Torah." The Torah is the Pentateuch, the Five Books of Moses. In our sacred tradition, The Torah is deemed to be the word of God, complete, perfect, and unchanging. By contrast, Torah refers to The Torah plus the entire world of meaning constructed upon it by successive generations of rabbinic teachers who have sought to apply the words of The Torah to the changing exigencies of existence, for which exigencies the words of The Torah, despite their accepted divinity and perfection, had in their literal form become increasingly dysfunctional. In this sense, "Torah" is another designation for our continuously unraveling Sacred Tradition.

In order to justify the stream of their applications—and therefore *de facto* alterations—of The Torah, the early rabbis argued that when God gave Moses the text of the five-book

Torah on Mount Sinai—the Written Torah, as it came to be called—God also gave him the Oral Torah, comprising the direction or principles for the application of the unalterable Word.

To complicate matters somewhat, the expression "The Torah" is frequently used in place of "Torah" to mean "The Torah plus Tradition." Yet a consideration of the context in which the expression is used will regularly remove all possibility of confusion.

The concept of Torah is elaborated by the rabbis with almost mystical overtones. The Midrash, under Platonic influence, claims that The Torah, i.e., The Torah plus Oral Torah, preexisted the creation of the universe, and even served God as a blueprint for the Creation. Indeed, the early rabbis and their successors regarded the Torah as the comprehensive guide to all meaningful living. They considered it to be the blueprint for all worthy law, the foundation for all true ethics, and the clew for all activity requisite for connection with God. Given this scope, the Torah necessarily embodies quantity of detail that is potentially infinite. Yet its informing principle is unmistakably simple. According to the Talmud (Sot. 14a), the beginning and end of the Torah, yes, its alpha and omega, is the practice of lovingkindness. The passage declares that the Torah, and implicitly the entire Tradition of Torah, begins and ends with exemplary acts of love and kindness by God Almighty: at the beginning of Genesis God clothes Adam and Eve, and at the conclusion of Deuteronomy God attends to the burial of Moses.

Indeed, the imitation of God in Judaism, and therefore its

highest spirituality, consists in the commitment of self through God to love and kindness toward individuals, toward humanity as a whole, toward life in its broadest manifestations, and toward the principles of our faith Torah as the vehicles for the actualization of this commitment.

Between this commitment and its actualization in the totality of life, the Torah charts paths for our action. These paths, combining the value of Torah and the experience of its past implementation, constitute our system of halakhah. In some Jewish circles, the word "halakhah" is utilized to denote a legal decision that is regarded as fixed law. Yet the word itself, derived from the Hebrew verb meaning "to go," means "path," or "way," or "procedure."

Halakhah provides the means for true Jewish spirituality. Authentic Jewish spirituality comprises more than a good feeling, and derives from more than random realizations of the beauty of manifold nature or the marvels of human experience. Through halakhah Jewish spirituality connects us to the divine at every moment, in every thought, with every step and every act. Reinforcing, on the one hand, the realization that nothing is devoid of God's presence and, on the other, the obligation incumbent upon all of us to illumine with God's presence all that is profane, the halakhah fills us with a spirituality that is simultaneously true to our sacred tradition and conducive to a wholesome and spiritually satisfying life.

Halakhah points us to this goal by a comprehension rather than a compartmentalization of life. Halakhah covers the home as well as the synagogue and private space as well as the public square. It includes aesthetics no less than ethics and divine worship no less than human service. And it requires all of these as indispensable coordinates for contact with the divine.

These coordinates are all coordinates of action rather than profession of belief. Implicit in Torah is the rejection of the proposition that one truly believes what one professes to believe. In Torah the only theology that counts is the theology deducible from one's life as a Jew.

In its inclusiveness, halakhah reveals another distinction of Jewish spirituality. Unlike the spiritual goals of other worldviews, Jewish spirituality cannot be attained by the individual apart from the community. Spirituality in Judaism involves corporate effort as well as individual initiative. The individual remains spiritually unfulfilled as long as the community is spiritually wanting.

Furthermore, even where not explicitly, halakhah supports the pursuit of all worthy disciplines of study and all implementations of these disciplines designed for the improvement of the world. Yet, above all these, halakhah emphasizes the indispensability of the study of Torah as the fountainhead of the values. In Judaism it is Torah which must inform all other study and all human activity. Through its promotion of the *kiddush ha-hayyim,* the sacralization or ennoblement of all life, Torah brings us closer to the heartbeat of the universe. Torah thus constitutes not only the name of our faith and the marrow of our sacred tradition. It constitutes as well the spiritual agenda of the Jew.

Etz Ḥayyim Hi:
It is a Tree of Life

Norman J. Cohen

The defining metaphor for the Jewish people is the Exodus from Egypt and the ensuing journey through the desert to the mountain and ultimately the Promised Land. On one level, it is the paradigm of the life journey of each and every one of us, as we move from Egypt, *Mitzrayim*—that is, *metzarim,* the narrow places, the places that oppress and limit us—to the openness of the desert and its potential for liberation. We, like our ancestors, must throw off the yoke of confinement, that which ties us to the purely material and immediate, and move into uncharted territory which offers a glimpse into eternity.

The crowning moment in the paradigmatic journey of our people took place at Mount Sinai. After having the yoke of

Egyptian oppression removed from us, we exercised our newly found freedom by accepting the Yoke of Heaven, or *malkhut shamayim*. This sealing of the covenant between ourselves and God should have been the culmination of our journey; it should have taken place at the end of the trek through the desert. Yet it occurred close to the outset of the forty-year sojourn in the wilderness, in the third month of the first year, and, we ask, Why? Why did God give the Torah to the people of Israel so early on in their journey, when they still must have been in utter shock from the events surrounding the escape from Egypt and the parting of the waters of the Red Sea?

Sinai, however, was never the ultimate goal. *Matan Torah*, God's revelation of Torah to Israel, was to be perceived not as an end but as a means. In order to survive the desert and somehow make their way to the Land of Israel, the people needed the redemptive vehicle of God's word. It was the Torah which would enable them to overcome the aridity of the desert, the moments of fear and doubt, and the loneliness of the journey.

The struggle for survival in the desert has a way of sapping all of one's belief and strength. No wonder then that only a short time after passing through the Red Sea, when they were inundated by its waters, which had cleansed them from the Egyptian experience and carried them closer to the Land of Israel, and when they had uttered their song of redemption to God (*Shirat ha-Yam*, Exod. 15:1–21), the Israelites found themselves without water (Exod. 15:22). Whatever they had experienced at the Red Sea, the sense of

God's presence and power, a moment of uplifting song, dissipated in the course of three short days in the heat of the desert sun.

We, like the Israelites of old, try to survive in the prosaic interval of our lives, in the long stretches between the rare moments of uplift that we feel. Like the Israelites, we search desperately for the source of our own salvation on the journey of our every day. We, too, long to reach the nearest oasis in the hope of drinking from its salvific waters.

Ironically, when the Israelites did come upon an oasis, its waters were too bitter to drink (Exod. 15:23). It, therefore, was called Marah (Bitterness). However, upon hearing the complaints of this fledgling people, Moses cried out for help to God, who showed him a tree, a piece of wood. And Moses took the wood and threw it into the water, which somehow transformed the bitter waters of Marah into waters of sweetness, waters of salvation (Exod. 15:24–25).

Commentators from Rashi onward have continually wondered about this miraculous tree whose wood could make the bitter waters sweet. As Gunther Plaut notes, trees like the oak contain tannin, which can neutralize the alkalinity of water, thereby causing the bitter matter to sink to the bottom.[1] Yet, if we do not take the text literally, understanding it instead to have symbolic power, then perhaps it is not important to know the type of tree intended by the biblical writer. The rabbis know this very well, as they demand that

---

1. Gunther Plaut, ed., *The Torah: A Modern Commentary* (New York: Union of American Hebrew Congregations, 1981), p. 497.

we listen to the words used by the biblical writer. The Exodus text does not read *va-yareihu etz,* "God showed Moses a tree," but *va-yoreihu etz,* which means, "God taught him a tree." And what tree might it have been that God taught him which enabled him to make the bitter waters sweet? Of course, it had to have been the Torah, the *Etz Ḥayyim,* the Tree of Life.[2] What allows the rabbis to interpret this narrative so symbolically? The words which immediately follow in the very same verse in the text (v. 25): "There God gave them a statute and ordinance," i.e., the Torah.

For the rabbis, as for us, the Torah is the vehicle that transforms the bitter waters into waters of salvation. In order to survive the desert journey and all of its trauma, in order to traverse the distance between Egypt and the Promised Land, we Jews have only one means at our disposal—the Torah given at Sinai, which we have carried with us in all of our sojourns. It is the *Etz Ḥayyim,* the Tree of Life, which can provide us with *mayyim ḥayyim,* the life-giving waters for which each of us searches.

To be sure, the forty-year journey through the desert was fraught with many moments of suffering and doubt for the Israelites. Even after their experiences at Marah as well as Sinai, they constantly complained about the lack of food and water and longed to return to the fleshpots of Egypt. Contentious and rebellious in the face of the hardships of their journey, they resorted to shaping an image of a golden calf which would guarantee that God was in their midst, at

---

2. Mekhilta de-Rabbi Ishmael, Vayassa 1.

the very moment that Moses was receiving the Torah. Even after the revelation at Sinai, the people of Israel continued to show their vulnerability and lack of faith, despite possessing God's commandments.

Yet most powerfully it was God's word that would enable them to survive, and even flourish as a people. They would experience the fresh, life-giving waters of the oasis and eventually reach the Promised Land of their ancestors, as God had guaranteed, if they would imbibe the power of the words of Torah which they possessed. One again, they would sing a song of redemption, as they had done at the shores of the Red Sea.

An Individual's Journey: The Blessing of Torah Study

As it was for the Israelites of the desert generation, so it is with each and every one of us, their progeny. We live through the heat and the aridity of our own circuitous journeys, in the hope of occasionally experiencing those moments of true spiritual uplift that can keep us going. Like them, we too come to Marah and find that the waters there are bitter, but we continue to believe that we will survive despite the frustration and anger.

My personal journey began as a child growing up in a liberal Orthodox home in New York City, attending Hebrew school five afternoons a week, and wondering why I couldn't play ball in the schoolyard like all of my other friends. Nevertheless, I actually enjoyed learning Hebrew, although I usually would not admit it to anyone, and I especially liked being able to participate in Shabbat and holiday services at our synagogue. The melodies used by our ḥazzan, which to this day filter in and out of my consciousness, and the way the rabbi and certain individuals in the congregation made me feel a part of the community probably account for the reason why attending services was never perceived as a chore. Shul became an oasis, a place where I was refreshed. And I drank the sweet waters of Torah and imbibed the sweet melodies of worship and felt something special. It was as if I were sitting at home when I was in shul, especially when I went with my grandfather.

My paternal grandfather, whom we affectionately called Shorty (he was all of four feet, ten inches tall), had everything to do with my Jewish feelings as a young teenager. The times I accompanied him to shul on Shabbat afternoon, sitting next to him during the *se'udah shelishit* (the mystical third meal of the Sabbath, which is understood as a taste of the messianic banquet) and the afternoon study session between *Minḥah* (the afternoon service) and *Ma'ariv* (the evening service), were mystical for me. I especially recall watching his face as the rabbi or some other person interpreted the text being studied in a particularly intriguing way. His face shone with a light that could only be described as that which emanated from Moses as he descended from Sinai (Exod. 34:29). It was obvious to me that he was transformed by the words of Torah which he had experienced, and all I wanted was to feel the same way as Shorty did.

Those moments studying midrashic texts or *Pirkei Avot*

with my grandfather's friends on Shabbat set me upon a path which was irreversible. I sensed even then just how important studying Torah would be for me, knowing indeed that it would become the focus of much of my religious experience.

My journey to serious study of Torah and to an earnest commitment to Jewish life was, however, to be rather indirect. Following my bar mitzvah, I became less enamored of the Orthodox synagogue which I had attended and somewhat disenchanted with the Hebrew high school in which I was enrolled. The narrowness of the approach to such issues as the need for people to choose what is important to them and the lack of openness to students who asked questions about basic theological assumptions dampened some of my enthusiasm for study and for Judaism (in this case Orthodox Judaism) in general. The result was that I dropped out of Hebrew high, opting instead to spend my free time in other ways.

The conduit back to Jewish involvement, however, surprised even me. Since some of my friends had begun to participate in a Zionist youth organization called Young Judea, I decided to join. I remember well the first meeting I attended; I was shocked to see my friends doing Israeli dancing, something I swore I would never try. But the upshot was that six months later I became a member of the National Young Judea Dance Group, which was followed by an ever increasing involvement in the movement. In looking back on those years, I still am amazed by the impact that YJ and the Zionist dream had upon me, and how it trans-

formed my life. The sheer joy I felt as a Jew who loved
Israel and resonated with the vision of a Jewish state was
(and still is) indescribable.

My Young Judea experiences led me to Israel during my
junior year in college, where I continued as a chemistry
major at the Hebrew University. A funny thing happened,
however, on the way to Terra Sancta and the HU chem labs:
I realized that I enjoyed my classes in Hebrew literature and
classical Hebrew texts much more than my science courses.
The immersion in text study during that year in Israel
impelled me to change my academic focus when I returned
to the States. I became a Hebrew studies major and continued on in a master's program following graduation. I finally
had begun truly to understand the passion my grandfather
had for grappling with Jewish texts, and I was bent on
spending my life doing just that. My study and teaching at
the Hebrew Union College–Jewish Institute of Religion has
given me the opportunity to share my love of Torah with
many others, just as Shorty did with me.

I remember the first paper that Rabbi Borowitz assigned
to us in the introductory course in modern Jewish philoso-
phy/theology. It was entitled, "How Do I Experience God's
Presence?" After struggling with the topic for some time and
trying to characterize how I felt when I prayed and how (or
even if) prayer helped me to sense God's presence, I realized that more than in any other context, it was in the exhilaration of studying Torah and trying to find personal
meaning that I felt a true sense of both grounding and uplift
at the very same time. For me, Talmud Torah is the path to

sensing a closeness with the divine; with feeling the Shekhi-
nah's presence. By imbibing the power and the beauty of
the words of Torah, in finding insight into who I am and
what I can become, by becoming one with the text, I too,
found my way of transforming the bitter waters of Marah.

Between Moments of Pain and Faith

The journey through life is never smooth. It is fraught not
only with the day-to-day problems of making ends meet,
confronting the challenges associated with our professions,
and working at our relationships with those whom we love,
but also with the pain of illness, tragedy, separation, and
loneliness. These experiences frequently dominate our
lives; they can set the tone for the whole journey.

As it is with all of us, my life journey has been like the
trek through the desert which the Israelites experienced.
There have been times of heightened joy and exaltation,
moments of poetry and beauty, but they do not come every
day. The test, in truth, is how to survive and make the best
of all those prosaic moments in between.

In fact, my personal path has been marked by four major
events which brought me great pain. Four times have I
come to Marah and tasted the bitterness of the water; there
my faith in life's essential goodness and in the reality of the
power that makes for wholeness has been challenged.

While I was still a rabbinic student at the College–Institute, my mother died of cancer at a relatively young age.
Her extended suffering over several years, the physical pain

she had to endure, and the toll it took on her were very difficult for me to witness. After all, I knew her to be a wonderfully warm, sensitive, and most giving person, and she surely did not deserve what life had meted out to her. There were moments when I could not understand why this had happened to her. (I surely felt like the Israelites in the desert when they wondered why they had been brought out to the desert to experience death.) During that period, what I found most comforting was my study at the College–Institute. It provided me with a grounding that allowed me to see things in a larger perspective. The worldview of our traditional texts, which emphasizes the importance of each individual and the place of each person in the continuum of the human experience, made me realize how much my mother had given us. She touched my soul in the deepest way and was a most powerful model of integrity, warmth, and humility for me. In fact, she was the one who encouraged me to apply to rabbinic school, and that experience gave me a great deal of desperately needed sustenance. Studying Torah at HUC–JIR nourished my soul at a time of doubt and anger. I would even say that writing my rabbinic thesis while my mother was in the final months of her life literally kept me going, though the journey was so dark.

I had the same basic feeling while going through the trauma and pain surrounding the breakup of my first marriage. In the bleakest moments, when I was most disheartened and all I had to look forward to most days was returning to my small sublet with its rented furniture and its windows facing the gray wall of the apartment building on the next block, I craved the comforting haven of my class-room. The joy of studying and teaching allowed me at one and the same time to feel my passion for life, to connect in a basic way with other people, and (most of all) to regain a sense of purpose and focus. The most difficult moment in the entire process of separation and divorce was probably the day I left permanently the home in which my first wife and I lived with our three young children. The irony, how-ever, was that I had to teach an adult education class in a local synagogue that very evening. And almost miracu-lously I found that the pain of crossing that threshold and moving on to a new and frightening place in my life was somewhat lessened when I became immersed in a midrash that touched my very soul and gave me hope. Like the chil-dren of Israel when they set out into the desert, not know-ing with any certainty if they would survive but hopeful that God would lead them to an oasis, I could only think of the prophet's words: "All who are thirsty come to [drink of] the water" (Isa. 55:1). The words of Torah, and those who rel-ished the study of Torah, refreshed me when I most need-ed it.

I have never ceased wondering how at any given moment of Torah study the text has jumped off the page and taught me about myself as a human being. This was certainly true all the years that my father suffered as a stroke victim and I struggled with the burden of watching him bear his pain and trying to be there for him. The stories of char-acters like Esau responding to his father Jacob's needs when he became dependent upon his son in his old age, while

Jacob was nowhere to be found (Gen. 27), Joseph's willing-
ness to respond to his father's request that he visit his brothers in Shechem even though it was fraught with potential
pain (Gen. 37), and Isaac and Ishmael coming together at
the cave of Machpelah to bury their father Abraham (Gen.
25) became mirrors of my own life during the years of my
father's infirmity and subsequent death. Immersing myself
in these ancient biblical stories and filtering them through
the prism of my life experience helped me to understand
better who I was as a son and brother, and what my life
journey as part of a family was all about.

Similarly, when our seventeen-year-old son Ilan was
stricken with lymphocytic leukemia, and I thought that
everything in which I believed was shattered the moment
this innocent child began to suffer the pain of his treat-
ments, one source of real solace came from the community
of students and teachers of Torah of which I am blessed to
be a part. The darkness and fright of those early days of
Ilan's illness were dispelled by the warmth of a community
committed to Torah, just as the words which Israel received
at the mountain enabled them to traverse the perils of the
forty-year journey. The caring that I felt from my students
and colleagues at the college taught me about how a
community can provide spiritual nourishment to its members. The individuals studying to be rabbis, cantors, and
educators at the college, and the faculty privileged to share
their love of Torah with them, became a well of comfort and
strength for me. Every day they shared with me the power
of their belief in God, the source that makes for healing and

wholeness, and for that I will be ever grateful. They helped to lift my spirits by being living vehicles of Torah and its optimistic view of the world.

We Each Need a Teacher, a Mentor

I learned that we can neither navigate the bitter waters nor survive the arid sands of the desert by ourselves. In Moses, the Israelites had a model of faith and action, and a mentor and advocate who taught them that they could take the first steps into the Red Sea and survive. At moments of heightened fear and anger, Moses showed them how to find salvific waters in the midst of the parched desert. All of us, even those of us who are privileged to serve others in the Jewish community, need to feel the guiding presence of individuals who by virtue of their own life journeys can affirm for us that a path does exist and that we have the ability to find our own way.

I have been exceedingly lucky in my life. My grandfather, Reb Ḥayyim Barukh, Shorty, taught me not only what it was to be a passionate, devoted, and practicing Jew, but he touched my soul with his love of Torah. In so doing, he helped me to shape the course of my life and find supreme joy through the study of God's words. Likewise, several of my teachers at the Hebrew Union College–Jewish Institute of Religion, among them Rabbi Eugene Borowitz, modeled for me what a life of Torah is all about. They exemplified how a Jew had to live if the words of Torah resonate through one's being, while enabling me to find my own path and expression. They extended their hands to me, thus strengthening my own. As Moses empowered his people by word and deed, so, too, my teachers and my students have given me gifts of self which have shown me the way from one oasis to another. The waters of Marah need not remain bitter if we are fortunate to be touched by individuals of faith and caring.

With that debt of gratitude in mind, I dedicate this essay to Rabbi Eugene B. Borowitz on the occasion of his seventieth birthday. It is dedicated with much reverence and affection. For over twenty-five years, I have benefited from his wisdom, insight, spiritual passion, concern, and guidance. I am proud to say that he is my teacher, colleague, and friend.

Random Observations
on Spirituality

A. Stanley Dreyfus

After having scanned the invitation to write on spirituality, I was minded to respond prudently—by declining straight away. In the first place, spirituality, however the concept is interpreted, belongs to the private, rather than to the public domain. Secondly, my views on the subject are as transitory as Jonah's gourd; they are amended very frequently. Furthermore, I do not want to have to defend my opinions, tentative as they are, against allegations that they are superficial or heterodox—as indeed they may very well be. And, finally, I am reluctant to assume the risk of disrupting another's faith and propelling him or her, forfend, in the direction of *tarbut ra'ah*.

Yet, only a few minutes later, as I was about to discard his letter, I chanced to encounter Rabbi Joshua Saltzman, and his gentle persuasion induced me to reconsider. Then, that very night, while slogging through the mire cast up by a single mail delivery, I came upon three items that convinced me to rescind what I had supposed to be an irrevocable decision.

The first of these was a feature article in a Jewish newspaper. In it the author writes of the spiritual satisfaction she gained from joining a *chevra kadisha* in a California city. She had overcome her initial repugnance toward attending the dead after she had attended a Buddhist meditation retreat. That is somewhat unusual preparation for a Jewish ritual, since Buddhists dispose (or used to dispose) of bodies by means of burial, or by cremation, or by exposure to the elements. The latter two are not sanctioned by traditional Judaism. We are told that after *tahorah* had been performed and the woman shrouded, the members of the *chevra* each took soil from Israel and scattered it over the body, "dusting her closed eyes, heart and genitals." Having searched the sources unsuccessfully for any reference to this curious practice of scattering dirt upon the private parts, I conclude that we have here an instance of how Jewish tradition is fabricated and incorporated into the California *minhag*. But to continue. The *chevra* was then summoned "to pray to the deceased person, to ask for forgiveness if we had done anything to hurt or offend her . . . . We [also] said a prayer that asked for the woman's blessing and protection. . . . The final prayer . . . . invites the angels to watch over the person in all her paths and asks that no evil come before her." Surely these ministrations and devotions are an expression of genuine spirituality for some, but not for me.

Next, a synagogue bulletin announces a Spirituality Conference. "A major question for today's Reform Jewry"—it begins—"is what happens to people after they die." To be sure, the Reform Jews I meet do not appear to be obsessed by this "major question," but no doubt the organizers of the Conference are relying upon their own surveys. The speaker, it is promised, "will delve into the ramifications of immorality [*sic*], reincarnation and faith." Indeed. I had thought that only two Jews in all our history could discuss this topic out of personal experience. The resurrection of one of them constitutes the central dogma of our daughter religion, and the other is Isaac, later called the Patriarch, who, as a midrash has it, died upon the altar his father had built upon Mount Moriah, and was then miraculously restored to life. (Some anticipate the speedy return of the late Lubavitcher Rebbe, but we may hope that Reform Jews are not to be found among their number.) It would be far more salutary for the Spirituality Conference to take the misprint as literally inspired, and to investigate the immorality rampant in our society, leaving speculation on reincarnation to the adherents of the Eastern religions.

Finally, a British periodical reports the appointment of a rabbi to take charge of a program just inaugurated by the Reform movement of the United Kingdom. The Director intends to address one of their "newest areas," namely, "faith and spirituality—what it means to be Jewish for

individuals and for communities." Yet surely the rabbi is
aware that spirituality is not a Johnny-come-lately topic
among the Queen's Jewish subjects, and especially among
the non-Orthodox segment thereof. The report sent me to
my shelves in search of a long-dormant volume, with the
no-nonsense title *Jewish Addresses Delivered at the Services
of the Jewish Religious Union, 1902–3,* but the eighteen sermons are impassioned reactions to deeply-felt needs. They
were preached to people who had grown impatient with
the conventional mode of worship offered in the *fin de siècle* British synagogues, and who urgently sought ways by
which a genuine spirituality might be cultivated. The Rev.
Morris Joseph, Senior Minister of the West London Synagogue, declared in their behalf:

> What we want in this age is the religious spirit. Our need is
> not merely to talk about God, but to know Him and to feel
> Him, to have Him in our life, to see in Him what the Psalm-
> ist could call our 'salvation,' our one help, our one hope,
> our one joy. We want to get rid of this heavy weight of
> worldliness which is dragging us down to tear asunder this
> veil of self-love which is hiding realities from us. We want
> new ideals, a new philosophy of life, new life. . . . Let us
> regain our grasp on the highest, and put low things back
> into their rightful place; let us begin to pray once more, to
> pray in the submissive spirit of the saintly men of olden
> times, biblical and post-biblical, and we shall be safe. Our
> religious life will be safe; the religion of our fathers will be
> safe.

There is no novelty in Morris Joseph's words. Similar sentiments could be quoted from a host of Jewish pietists who preceded or followed him. The fostering of spirituality has always been a prime aim of the synagogue, and so it remains today. Yet our spirituality must be less concerned with achieving the *unio mystica,* less concerned with fostering strict observance of the ritual *mitzvot,* and greatly concerned with attracting the alienated, with relieving poverty and suffering, with transfusing hope into the hopeless.

My first intimations of spirituality came in my early childhood, when my parents brought me into the sanctuary of the Reform Congregation Rodef Sholom of Youngstown, Ohio. Week after week, listening to our rabbi's intoning the sonorities of the *Union Prayer Book* or the Torah and Haftarah lessons in the lilting accents of his Welsh boyhood, I fancied that the pronouncements of the Hebrew prophets must have resounded as awesomely as did Dr. Philo's. The service, formal and austere, replicated the style of the Protestant churches that Youngstown's "best people" attended, but Jews were then experimenting with a *minhag America,* trying to devise a form of spirituality that could address the extraordinary needs of the new community, and they found a not unworthy model in the dignified worship and the hushed reverence that were the hallmark of mainline Protestantism. Indeed, our prayer book appropriated some of the rubrics of the Christian liturgy: Minister, Choir, Responsive Reading, Sanctification, Adoration, Canticle, Anthem, Benediction. Much of our music was composed by Christians. Often the anthems were Protestant chorales, and the identical solos were sung in church of a Sunday, and in the Temple of a Sabbath. On Yom Kippur, at the Afternoon Service, *Etz Chayyim* was sung to an aria from Tosca, and the somber mood of the Memorial Service was established by Chopin's Funeral March, without compromising the Jewishness of the Day. People, it seems to me, wept more freely in the era of "Classical" Reform than they do today, and their venting of their emotions attested to their spirituality.

This early habit of attending Temple every Shabbat eve and morning makes me uncomfortable when illness or travel compel me to miss a service. Yet I do not regard myself as an especially prayerful person, although for many years I have taken great satisfaction in the study of the liturgy. There is, of course, a vast chasm between looking into the history and theology of *Siddur* and *Maḥzor* on the one hand, and, on the other, of uniting with a congregation in prayer. Sometimes the liturgy, read or sung, commands my full attention; more often, my thoughts range widely, neither trammeled nor restrained by the prayer book in my hands. Franz Rosenzweig is reported to have said, "All of a sudden, when you are reading the prayer book, a word comes alive," and so it often happens for me. Something in the Gates series that I had first seen in manuscript, perhaps had helped to rework, and had read hundreds of times afterwards, can unexpectedly reveal a truth that I had never before discerned. Still, whether I follow the service closely or meander from it, it is in the synagogue, in company with other Jews, that I become most receptive to the spiritual. For in the course of public worship, as Benjamin Jowett (1817–93), the Oxford Platonist, remarked:

we may pause for a moment in our journey that we may proceed refreshed. Here we are raised above the mere thoughts of mankind; we hear words of the saints and prophets of old; we live for a short time in the nearer companionship of God and of another world; we pass in review the last few days, and ask ourselves whether we are doing enough for others; we seek to realize in our minds a higher standard of duty and character. Here are revived in us those aspirations after another and better state of being, which in good men are always returning, and are never completely satisfied, but which, like wings, bear us up on the sea of life, and prevent our sinking into the routine of custom which prevails in the world around us. Here we resign ourselves to the pure thought, to the pure will, to the pure mind, which is the truer part of our own souls, and in which and through which we see God. It would be foolish to maintain that we should always be attending to the words of the service, or that our thoughts may not wander to our own individual circumstances. One advantage of public worship is that it is also private; any reasonable act of devotion may form part of it; we may offer up to God our studies, entreating Him to give us the power to use our natural talents that they may be the instruments of His service. We may consecrate to Him our business, praying that the gains we make may be employed in His service, and sometimes devising plans of charity and philanthropy. We may review our thoughts, begging Him . . . to infuse into us a new mind and character. . . .

For me, spirituality is enhanced when the service is conducted by a rabbi who adheres to the traditional liturgical rubrics, and who, in leading the prayers, conveys the *perush hamillot* without at the same time turning the bima into a classroom. Likewise, I prefer a cantor who is praying rather than performing, who is partial to the great masters of Jewish music, Sulzer, Lewandowski, and the likes of them, and who is assisted by a well-trained choir and accompanied by a competent organist. My spirituality is diminished when I am in a congregation where liberties are taken with the text of the prayer book in the name of a "gender-sensitive" liturgy. It is likewise diminished by the revival of long-discarded practices and mannerisms that to my mind bespeak doubts about the authenticity or the adequacy of Reform Judaism as it has come down to us. That is, of course, a personal opinion, and it is not intended as a reflection on the allegiance or the judgement of those who find spirituality in the rediscovery of traditional modes.

* * *

I encounter spirituality not only when I join in the statutory services of the synagogue, but also when I work at construing a Hebrew text in my study. The struggle to penetrate into the various levels of the text becomes itself a gratifying spiritual exercise, even though the content of the document often resonates with outmoded concepts and often perpetuates old and vicious animosities which are better forgotten. These do not provide grist for spirituality. Certainly ours is not the first generation to question, or to ignore, or openly to reject certain of the *mitzvot* enjoined by the Torah. Even those who look forward most eagerly to the advent of Messiah do not go about proclaiming their intent to restore capital punishment for the child who curses his parents, nor even for adultery, although some dwell wistfully upon the reestablishment of the sacrificial cult and the restoration of priestly prerogatives. It is the glory of Reform that it never hesitated to abandon doctrines and to discard practices that reason determined to be no longer conducive to spirituality, but rather impediments to attaining it.

* * *

The death notices published in the morning newspaper remind me that I have lived longer than many of those whose obituaries are recorded there. Why this privilege has been granted me, I cannot imagine. "We are powerless," the Mishnah asserts, "to account either for the prosperity of the evildoers, or for the lowly state of the righteous." Nor, for that matter, can we explain the reverse. Mine has been the great good fortune of having been born to caring and intellectually gifted parents, of having been reared with affectionate siblings, of winning and retaining the love of the most exemplary woman, the mother of our two sons, of watching them attain responsible maturity in years when many of their contemporaries seemed bent upon destroying themselves and their society. Mine has been the good fortune to see our sons take on careers that would benefit others as well as themselves, to see them marry women of superlative grace and character, and in their turn bring forth a new generation, rich in promise. Mine has been the extraordinary fortune to have had demanding teachers, brilliant colleagues, a goodly number of responsive congregants, a coterie of loyal and magnanimous friends. After enumerating such benefits, my Alsatian forebears would have hastily added *umberufen un' umbeschrien,* "May all this not attract the notice of the demons!" I will not regard that as a reliable means of averting evil, nor can I endorse the popular adage, *Hakol talui bemazal,* "Everything depends on luck." Enough that in the face of the *razei olam,* the eternal mysteries, my doubts and mundanity willy-nilly give way to spirituality, manifesting itself both in deepest gratitude for a myriad of blessings, and in a firm resolve to enhance the lives of those with whom my own life has been intertwined, during the time that remains to me. "God of the morning, noon, and evening of my life when the day is fierce with heat, may I find the comfort of Your shade. When the day dims, let the light I have kindled abide."

Reform Religious Zionism: Celebrating the Sacred in Time and Space

Lawrence A. Hoffman

I attended my first Zionist convention in 1954. As the car driving me there trundled over old two-lane highways stretching endlessly, it seemed, through the southern Ontario countryside, my driver and I struggled to make conversation. He was, after all, a somewhat elderly man (I thought) whom I had never met, and I was only twelve years old. He was a Zionist himself, naturally, so he went on enthusiastically about the new State of Israel, to which I, incipient adolescent that I was, inquired what my adult mentor in Zionism would do if the state were inexplicably to fail. Matter-of-factly, he announced, "First of all, it won't; it can't; but if the state were to fail [did he really use the

59

subjunctive mood?], I wouldn't be here; I would gladly die first."

Such was the Zionist passion that surrounded my youth—in the form of an ongoing adult conversation into which I merely wandered in and out. By contrast, some twenty-five years later, Israel's past president, Ephraim Katzir, convinced five academicians (myself among them) to establish a North American Zionist think tank, because (he said), "No one talks about Zionism any more. European cafes were once packed with idea-intoxicated Jews who spoke only of Herzl, a Jewish state, and the like. Not any more."

It had recently occurred to me that the very locution, "idea-intoxicated Jew," is becoming an oxymoron; we are all being increasingly pressured to become mere programmers. In 1959, Arthur Hertzberg could write a book called *The Zionist Idea*. That was when "Zionist" was a living adjective, and "idea" a living noun. Our generation's parallel book would be named, "How to Plan the Perfect Israel Program."

I hold that ideas matter more than programs. It follows then that Zionism must be a matter for the mind. We ought to come to terms with Zionism as more than a youth group junket; Zionism must once again be an idea that moves us.

But what is Zionism? It is many things, of course, but whether political, cultural, practical, or theological, Zionism presupposes something unnatural, unhealthy, or unredemptive about Jewish life without a Jewish state. Ideological Zionism, for instance, generally presupposes a metaphysical condition called *galut;* it summons us to trade in this metaphysical exile for Israeli citizenship. A political spin on *galut* as a theological category is political Zionism's dogma that predicates antisemitism in the world outside—antisemitism as a metaphysical condition, mind you, like a chronic disease: if dormant today, it will resurface tomorrow.

There is a reason we Reform Jews have eschewed Zionist discussion. It is not that we are not Zionists; we are! But we lack the terms to talk about it. Zionist theory is largely troublesome for us, because much as we want to retain Israel as a theological realia, we reject the metaphysics on which prior claims for doing so have traditionally depended. Most of us simply do not want to cash in the diaspora as so many devalued chips left over from a bad bet with history.

But if Zionism is an *idea,* it need not be equated with specific claims left over in the annals of Zionist literature. It lets us start all over again. We are like shipwrecked swimmers born aloft in the sea by the remnants of a raft. We discover that we have not drowned even though the raft disappeared several years ago. We can either decide that without the raft we are really drowning, in which case we agree to go under, or we can begin the search for whatever it is that now miraculously keeps us afloat. We are still afloat with Zionism, our passion for a Jewish state. If the old raft of classical Zionist thought, a denial of the diaspora and faith in antisemitism, no longer works, we need to launch a search for whatever will work to keep us afloat as Zionists in the troubled waters of our time.

Zionism, then, is not like Hegelian philosophy, say, or talmudic study, where proper conversation begins either with

Hegel or with the Talmud, and then becomes one more chapter in an ongoing conversation about a root literary corpus. It is instead more like medieval metaphysics, in that it is an ongoing fascination with the human place in the world, but in this case, the Jewish place in a world which contains among other things something utterly inalienable and absolutely irreducible, something called *eretz yisrael*. So my first positive contribution to the definition of Zionism is this:

We are Zionists if we raise *eretz yisrael* to the same theoretical level of importance as the three other irreducible realities that we take for granted because they also cannot be argued, proved, or demonstrated, but only assumed as the ground of our Jewish being—namely: God, Torah and *am yisrael*. Moreover, as long as history is as it is, *eretz yisrael* must also be *medinat yisrael*.[1]

We were all once taught these three irreducible essences in our metaphysical map of reality: God, Torah, and Israel (the People). *Yisrael ve-oraita ve-kudsha berikh hu—ḥad hu;* but why privilege God, Torah, and People over Land? Land is hardly inconsequential—it is ubiquitous in our tradition. Halakhah requires a *milḥemet mitzvah* (war of reli-

---

1. The literature, of course, begins only with the vision of statehood, so it is tempting to define the metaphysical entity in question as *medinat yisrael,* not just *eretz yisrael*. Indeed, I fully agree that a modern metaphysician who abandons the idea of a Jewish state flies in the face of Zionist thought. But I begin with the notion of a Jewish land and only thereby arrive at the idea of a Jewish state there. That is precisely the route that the early Zionists who abandoned a Uganda project took. So relationship to the state must depend on a prior commitment to the Land.

gious obligation) to defend it. From Deuteronomy to the original *Arami oved avi* midrash in the Passover Haggadah,[2] Exodus from Egypt and entry to our Land were inseparable—the first supplied "people," the other, "Land," and in the middle there was Sinai, that is, "Torah," all three being signs of God. To ignore Land as a fourth corner of our faith is akin to the sleight of hand by which a secular Jew omits God, while accepting only people and Torah. Zionism, then, is the insistence on the brute fact of *eretz yisrael* as metaphysically necessary. Zionist debate is a branch of Jewish metaphysics: a rambling conversation about the role of a thing called *eretz* in the fabric of Jewish being.

Proper Zionist thought begins, therefore, with a consideration of what it means to be a landed people; with what must follow from adding a fourth term to the big three, arriving at this necessary quaternity at the core of Judaism: God, Torah, Israel (the people), and Israel (the land).

But our Zionism must be religious and Reform, or it will be someone else's, not "ours." In my days with the Zionist think tank, I learned that even though all metaphysicians may have something in common, they cannot all automatically do metaphysics together. It is helpful for Platonists and Aristotelians to separate into peacefully coexistent schools of thought, on occasion to read each other's material (even if only to fulminate about their opponents' vapidity), but then to do their business in groups of like-minded col-

---

2. On which, cf. Daniel Goldschmidt, *Haggadah shel Pesaḥ ve-Toldoteha* (Jerusalem: Mosad Bialik, 1960), introduction; and Lawrence A. Hoffman, *Beyond the Text* (Bloomington: Indiana University Press, 1987), pp. 90–101.

leagues. My think tank failed me because it insisted on the romantic notion that when we say with tradition, *Kol yisrael arevim zeh va-zeh* ("all Jews are bound together in mutual dependence"), or as secular UJA rhetoric would have it, "We are One," it means that Zionism unifies us to the point where other intellectual or ethical differences disappear. They never do. To ask Reform Jews to do Zionism as if religion or Reform were secondary is like asking Jews in New York or Chicago to discuss American constitutional law as if their Jewishness were not tied up in First Amendment rights, or asking women to overcome their gender experience in the higher cause of rabbinic Judaism. This higher-cause argument is endemic to intellectual imperialism, and we Reform Jews are ready targets for the imperialism of traditionalists who tell us to check our liberalism at the door of Jewish life; or for secularists who ask us to set aside our concern for religious equality or civil rights in the interest of a united Zionist front. It won't work. My second lesson, then, is that we need a Reform religious Zionism or we shall have no Zionism at all.

Where, then, must Reform religious Zionism as an idea that matters begin? We have learned from Eugene B. Borowitz that religion enters with our covenant with God, and Reform emerges with the insistence on a self, albeit what he calls now a postmodern self in which pure individual autonomy disappears as illusory. I have no essential quarrel with either, though I have my own version of both.

Borowitz links Zionism to the covenant on the grounds that peoplehood requires land and a land requires a state. In an address to the Central Conference of American Rabbis to which this paper was a response, he said, "My Zionism is a direct outgrowth of my religious belief about the people of Israel. . . . [In fact] the intensity of one's Reform Zionism is correlated to the importance we attach to the people of Israel in our faith."[3] Zionism and landedness is thus for him merely *derivative* of peoplehood and covenanthood. But one can be passionate about both without arriving at Zionism—as the Satmar Hasidim (whom he cites) demonstrate. There is nothing innately illogical about religious territorialism, a religious version of Israel Zangwill, perhaps, whose faith might equally have led to Zionism or not, but whose commitment to *am yisrael* could in neither case be doubted. By contrast, I have raised landedness to primacy, making it axiomatic as part and parcel of Jewish covenanthood. For me, there is God, Torah, Israel (the people), and Israel (the land); none of the four is dispensable. I invoke Harry Orlinsky, *zikhrono livrakhah,* who taught us all that, biblically speaking, *eretz yisrael* is intrinsic to the covenant—not merely logically derived from it.[4]

As for Reform, I think it clear that Reform is inherently religious, and it is so because it cares centrally for God. But what is there about God that has so fascinated Reform Jews? Not God as creator, revealer, or redeemer, though we accept

---

3. Eugene B. Borowitz, "What is Reform Religious Zionism," *CCAR Yearbook,* vol. 104, 1994, p. 74.
4. See his "Biblical Concept of the Land of Israel: Cornerstone of the Covenant Between God and Israel," in *Land of Israel: Jewish Perspectives,* ed. Lawrence A. Hoffman (Notre Dame: University of Notre Dame Press, 1986), pp. 27–64.

all three. No, for Reform Jews, God emerged as the sole guarantor of holiness. If Reform has done anything, it has accomplished this: it has mandated holiness as the end of human endeavor. Reform Jews recognized that *kodesh* versus *ḥol* is an essential binary opposition that has driven all of Jewish thought from the Bible until our time.[5] They tended to accept or to reject halakhah depending on whether it supported or ran contrary to holiness. Following Holdheim,[6] they did away with Shabbat work regulations precisely because they felt that the essence of Shabbat was the sacred.[7] We replaced the traditional Yom Kippur reading of the *arayot* (the biblical list of illicit sexual relationships) with Leviticus 19, *kedoshim tihyu* ("You shall be holy . . . "). We have made short shrift of much of the *Tefillah,* but not the *Kedushat Hashem,* which we have outfitted with one stirring musical setting after another. Reform Judaism has thus systematically insisted on the sacred as the goal of human life. Moreover, as to holiness and its manifestations in human conduct, it cannot be denied that Reform has systematically emphasized universal ethics, so that a Reform Zionism, while particularistic, may not on that account also be ethically parochial. And finally, Reform has emphasized the fulcral role of the morally responsible and existentially determinative self—a matter to which I will return shortly.

5. See Hoffman, *Beyond the Text,* pp. 20–45.

6. See Gunther Plaut, *The Rise of Reform Judaism* (New York: World Union for Progressive Judaism, 1963), pp. 192–195.

7. See Lawrence A. Hoffman, "The Jewish Sabbath Faces Modernity," in *The Sabbath in Jewish and Christian Tradition,* ed. Tamara Eskenazi (New York: Crossroad, 1991).

For now, however, I can summarize by saying that Reform religious Zionism will have to accommodate these equally critical components: first, from Zionism's essence, our inherent landedness as a people; second, from religion, landedness raised to primacy because of God but along with and equal to Torah and Israel (the people); and third, from "Reform," the primacy of individual conscience, universal ethics, and the commitment to pursue holiness as the end of human life.

Finally, then, I turn to the self, using my own perspective as a liturgist.

The particular version of the self I invoke is a ritual self. Long before postmodernism, ritualists posited the essentially social nature of the individual, and the inability to encounter objective reality without the mediation of interpretation. More than rational animals, we humans are at our core *interpretive* animals, demanding interpretation of everything from the food we eat to the dreams we concoct.[8] Tradition is the word we use to describe the carrier of our age-old and brand-new multiple-layered interpretations.[9] To be a Jew is to conceptualize ourselves as weavers for whom the present moment is just the newest stitching in the tapestry of Jewish interpretation. We interact with the world of our senses by shaping it according to the threads, the patterns,

---

8. See, e.g., R. A. Sharpe, *Contemporary Aesthetics: A Philosophical Analysis* (New York: St. Martin's Press, 1983).

9. See Lawrence A. Hoffman, "What Is a Liturgical Tradition?" in *The Changing Face of Jewish and Christian Worship in North America,* ed. Paul F. Bradshaw and Lawrence A. Hoffman (Notre Dame: University of Notre Dame Press, 1991), pp. 3–25.

and the colors of our Jewish past, which (as it were) we pull into our present. This is, above all, a ritual task.

For Reform Jews (for whom the sacred is primary), that means ritualizing, and thus bringing into being, our encounter with the holy. For Zionists (as we shall see), it means, specifically, the holy as applied to space.

A few words then on how we ritualize sacred space, which I illustrate first with a brief thought on time.[10]

Pressed between the urgent bookends of a biography that may turn out to have fewer chapters than we plan on, we human beings unconsciously structure life as if it were a video tape, passing frame by frame through the window of our consciousness. In this model, memory is what is left of yesterday's movie show. But suppose the physicists are right when they tell us that time and space are a single continuum, differing only in metaphorical use. Time, for example, "passes"; space does not.

Now, unlike human beings, God is *not* time-bound. The rabbis treat even God's memory, therefore, not temporally, but *spatially*. Picture God's universe, then, not as a video in time, but as infinite space, where everything happens simultaneously. We humans have access to a single limited quadrant of space that we call our present. But God sees it all— all of time/space at the same temporal/spatial moment. God lives in time the way humans live in space. It is all present to the mind of God, all at once.

---

10. For details, see Lawrence A. Hoffman, "Does God Remember?" in *Memory in Judaism and Christianity,* ed. Lawrence Cunningham and Michael A. Signer (Notre Dame: University of Notre Dame Press, 1996).

What all this has to do with religious Zionism is that human beings cannot see it "all at once"—a metaphor combining space ("all") and time ("at once"); only God, who is above time and space, can do that. We, by contrast, are beyond neither, but are gifted with the ability to ritualize our encounter with both. Religion, as we know it in the West, sanctifies time; Zionism sanctifies space. Judaism insists on the sacred potential of both dimensions; and that is why we need to be both religious and Zionist.

Religion thus gives us a sacred calendar, while Zionism provides a sacred map—each equally rich in ritual potential, because as interpretive beings, we encounter the world ritually, above all. Diasporan religion berates Israelis for letting even Yom Kippur go by unritualized. Israelis chastise us for being so geographically secularized as to live *ḥutz la-aretz.* Time-conscious diasporan Jews notice holy space primarily because things happened there in history; space-conscious Israelis mark their calendars with events that affected their country, their space. Therefore they keep Yom Ha-Zikaron but not necessarily Yom Kippur. Jews in the diaspora like to visit Hezekiah's tunnel or the City of David, but not necessarily the land qua land, the land of which A. D. Gordon wrote with all the passion that we reserve only for time. *Mutatis mutandis.* Only a diasporan Jew like Heschel could yearn above all for a sanctuary in time.

We have two liturgies too; the liturgy of time: *Shaḥarit* through *Ma'ariv,* daily; and the annual *maḥzor*—and the liturgy of space: pilgrimage to our Land; and for some, actually *living* there, in touch with the contours of its space the way diasporan Jews know the feel of sacred time. Diasporan Jews will have to learn to value aliyah as a sacred option, a celebration of the sacrality of space, prior to time. Israeli Jews will have to appreciate how we in the diaspora (if we are to remain Jewish at all) must be the primary guardians of time as they are of space.

One way or the other, the ultimate goal for Jews has been the messianic. Reform Judaism is messianic through and through, but its classical variety ignored the messianic vision of Zionism. As religious Zionists, we should link the messianic both to diasporan time and to Israeli space. Juxtapose our usual diasporan religious conceptual scheme of creation, revelation, and redemption with Zionism's exile and redemption. Redemption figures in both, but for religion it is a temporal thing that happens to occur in space, while for Zionism it is quintessentially a spatial phenomenon that happens to occur in time. Religious Zionism is thus that perspective wherein we strive for redemption in both space and time. As the route to the messianic end, Reform religious Zionism demands a universal ethic rooted in Jewish particularity; and it charges individuals with the ethical and ritual obligation to pursue holiness in space and time—indeed, insofar as reality is determined in part by our own action, we thereby do not pursue holiness so much as we actually *establish* the sacred as ontologically real in the dual space-time grid of being.[11] We hold out hope for redemption in our Land, but also in history.

11. The ethical is itself ritualized behavior. Instead of seeing ritual as an area of human activity that is subordinate to ethics, we ought to reconceptualize ethics as a subsection of ritual, namely, a ritualized way of relationship that establishes the sacrality of the other in the same way that rituals of liturgy establish the sacrality of time and space.

"This is Your Life": Reflections on Jewish Spirituality

Lawrence Kushner

This is Your Life

There used to be a TV show when I was growing up where they'd bring an unsuspecting soul out of the audience and tell his or her life story. It was creatively called *This is Your Life!* The master of ceremonies would begin telling the biography and then, from off stage, you typically might hear a little old lady say, "I remember the way you used to sit in the back row of my geometry class and throw paper airplanes at the little blonde girl across the aisle." Whereupon the guest of honor would say something like, "Oh my God, It's Mrs. Connley, my geometry teacher! And she would come out from behind the curtain and they would hug and sometimes cry. The emcee would tell a few more stories and introduce a few more mystery guests until

73

past joined present and the guest's life was told, and then
the show was over. It took a half-hour.

There is a fascinating passage near the very end of the
Torah in Deuteronomy 29:3–4: "And not until this day had
God given you a heart to understand, eyes to see, nor ears
to hear. I led you through the wilderness forty years; the
clothes on your back did not wear out." In other words, for
forty years we didn't know what was going on and never
once had to go to a tailor or a discount clothing store.
Seems odd.

Rabbi Simḥah Bunem of Przysucha explains that it means
that we did not understand any of the miracles God did for
us during the whole forty years.[1] They were all events
unique to that particular time. Because there had never
been anything like them before (nor will there ever be
again), we never figured out what was going on until it was
over. But on "this day" (today) the entire Torah is finished,
set in fixed form for the generations. And, get this, the
Torah has been made from the stories which make up our
very lives.

You may realize that the source of Jewish spirituality is
discovering that your ordinary life has been in the Torah all
along. And the reason the wilderness generation didn't
understand it while it was "coming" is that they were just
too busy living it! But then, at the end of the forty years
(and their lives? and ours?), they realized that all the teachings of the Torah had been clothed with their deeds, made

---

1. *Itturei Torah* VI, 172b.

from whatever they did. (I think this is what Simḥah Bunem meant when he said that the clothing didn't wear out.) And not just the holy moments either, but the ordinary, mundane, wayward, even sinful ones as well! Just imagine, ultimate truth and meaning clothed in the stories of your life! This is Your Life!

Now if you object that the deeds of your life are simply too ordinary, too irreligious, take comfort in the behavior of everyone from Adam through Joshua, that is, everyone in the Torah. Murderers, lechers, liars, cheats, thieves. (As Professor Hanan Brichto used to quip, there's no one in the Hebrew Bible you'd want your kid to grow up to be like.) And the wilderness generation, that wacky, zany band of irreligious forty-year wanderers—who with their own eyes saw the Red Sea split and Moses ascend Mount Sinai, ate manna for breakfast and quail for supper—these were the ones who built the golden calf, denied God at every opportunity, begged to go back to Egypt, and committed adultery with every neighboring tribe they met; these exemplary spiritual specimens were privileged to have the serial rights to their life story chosen as the script for the holiest document ever recorded. (So there's hope for you and me yet.)

No matter how pedestrian, no matter how exalted, no matter how shameful, no matter how holy, your life is magic, all your actions are lights. And they're all in the Torah. And when you receive the Torah you acknowledge the sanctity of your life story. Something just beneath the surface of everyday life shines through it, and, for a moment, the ordinary becomes sacred. Meaning is everywhere and we are blessed. In the words of Psalm 24, "The whole world is full of God."

Federal Express

The last thing an author gets to look at before he or she sees an actual finished book is a batch of stapled sheaves of book sections. They are called folded and gathereds, or simply, proofs.

Now people in the book business, like people in most businesses, are always looking for ways to make their jobs go quickly, so they often unceremoniously shorten the titles of books down to just a word or two. Since my book *God Was in This Place and I, I Did Not Know* may actually have one of the longer titles of any trade book ever published, it was an easy victim to such abbreviating. Eleven words. This usually gets abbreviated to simply, *God Was in This Place*. And, at least on one occasion, it was further distilled by a mail room clerk to just *God*. Now this is all a roundabout way of explaining how the Federal Express package that arrived at my home from the publisher was labeled "God Proofs."

My kids, who were home to sign for the package, telephoned me at the office at once to announce—not without some mischievous pleasure—that what I had been working and waiting for my whole adult life had just arrived via FedEx. "It's finally here, Dad, God Proofs." "Is there a return address?" I asked, wondering whether heaven has a ZIP code.

If a proof for God could come in the mail, what would it look like? I'll tell you. It would be a book containing all the ordinary stories of your life. Your own personal Torah. But, of course, if your life is part of the Torah, then there is something more to your life than just your life. There is something more to yourself than your self. At the core of your innermost self is something which is not yourself.

Self of the Universe

The late Professor Alexander Altmann once observed that "finding God and worshiping God is but another way of saying that we have found our Self . . . people are spiritually reborn in God, and God is, as it were, reborn in people."[2] That's where "God" comes in. God and self are intimately connected. You might say that spiritual encounters involve two selves, your self and the Self of the Universe.

We find ourselves in two places: in our innermost hearts and in the firmament overhead. But it is really the same. As in the words of the old Gnostic adage: "as within so without, as above, so below."

God is our sense of self, our innermost essence, encountered throughout all creation. Our selves are made of God's Self. But this does not mean that the world is our creation, or that we are God. It does mean that this awareness, this sense of uniqueness, we feel cannot possibly have come just from ourselves. It is bigger than us and must be in

---

2. See his "God and the Self," *Judaism* 3, no. 2 (1954): 146.

everyone else. In all living things. In mountains and water and fire. Everywhere.

Self is orchestration of awareness, integration of consciousness, what holds it all together, making it whole and able to be called by a single name—our name. Self is what integrates and unifies our physical body, our thoughts, our actions. It is the same with God and creation. The universe too has a name by which it means to integrate its myriad contradictions into one organism. The universe, like you and me, has a Self, a Self that nourishes and sustains each individual self. God is to being as the self is to us. God is the *Anokhi shel Olam,* the "I" of the world, the Self of the Universe.

One of my high school students once asked me if I could prove there was a God. Instead I asked her if she had a self. She thought for a moment and said, "Of course."

"And is your self important to you?"

"Very," she replied.

"And where would you be," I pushed, "without your self?"

"In big trouble."

"Can you prove you have one?"

She smiled. "I get what you mean."

Heaven on Earth

Classical Hebrew has no word for "spirituality." (The modern Hebrew *ruḥaniyut* comes from our English word.) The English word "spiritual" means immaterial and connotes the religious. The concept comes to us with the heavy baggage of Western culture dividing the universe into material and spiritual. For Judaism everything, including, and especially, such apparently not-spiritual and grossly material things as garbage, sweat, dirt, and bushes, is not an impediment to but a dimension of spirituality. Judaism understands that the business of religion is to keep this awesome truth ever before us. "The whole world is full of God" is a dimension of living in which we are continually aware of God's presence.

You already are where you need to be. You need go nowhere else. Feel now the moisture on your tongue. Sense the effortless filling and emptying of your lungs. See the involuntary blinking of your eyes. Find a point an inch or so behind your sternum where your heart beats. That is where the place is. Right here all along, and we did not know it because we were fast asleep, here in this very place. And for this reason we each have great power.

Starting Fires

Reb Yehudah Aryeh Leib of Ger, author of the great spiritual classic, *Sefat Emet,* says that religious acts cannot be accomplished by just personal strength alone; but rather, through the power of performing a religious act some higher kind of spiritual power is awakened. This is because the Holy One sets a spark in each one of us. And by means of devotion, like attracts like. The spiritual power in the deed and the spiritual power in the soul are roused.

Then the inner power awakens. It is all a matter of persever-
ance.

We must remember, he says, that sooner or later, anything
accomplished by the power of a human being must stop.
But when the power of the Holy One is awakened, this kind
of power continues forever. Whatever you do matters, but
nothing you do will matter very much unless you transcend
yourself, unless you join your deed to something beyond
yourself, or, as it is said, arouse the world on high. And if
you do, then whatever you do will endure.

In the language of the kabbalistic maxim: "By means of
the awakening below, comes the awakening on high." So,
not only do our acts awaken something on high and enable
us to transcend ourselves, our yearning awakens things on
high and within.

Death and Covenant

Except for the fact that the *mohel* was caught in traffic and
forty-five minutes late, and it was *erev Kol Nidrei,* it began
as any other *bris.* The physician was, of course, medically
excellent but also religiously elegant. He even held the
father's hand as the latter brought his son into the covenant
of Abraham our Father. The baby was terrific too. Barely a
cry. And by the time the brief procedure was done, the
infant had already closed his little eyes and was near sleep.
My eyes, as usual, were moist with tears.

The *mohel* nodded to me, as planned, to begin the *Kiddush,* which is when Jewish boys are named. Then I made
some joke about how as an act of compassion for the

assembled company, I was going to invite the two *ḥazza-nim* who were present to chant it instead. Everyone laughed. But before we could begin we suddenly realized that a man sitting in front of me had slumped over in his chair. His eyes were glassy, his mouth hung open, he was very pale. His wife screamed. I was sure he was having a heart attack, but the *mohel* knew better. He calmly handed me the baby and helped lay the man on the floor. He had only fainted. So not only had the baby survived the *bris,* but so had at least one other guest. The doctor elevated the man's feet and loosened his necktie, and in no time the man was conscious and able to share an embarrassed smile. But I couldn't get it out of my head that for a minute this poor kind man had died and been reborn.

So I offered a short *devar* on the baby's name. I remember that one of the things I said was that the only people who have life are those who understand how frail and precious it truly is. And all the while I spoke, a man lay on the floor at my feet and this new little Jewish soul I held in my arms was fast asleep.

This may be what Mendel of Vorki meant when he said that "to be a human being requires silent screaming, upright kneeling, and motionless dancing."

Riding the Golden Camel

I am over on the Mount of Olives maybe ten, fifteen years ago. We have come to see that magnificent view of the Old City and indulge some people in our party, whose hearts

are set on a camel ride. We watch them get their money's
worth of thrills as the beast lurches first up and forward,
then higher and backward, and finally forward and towering
level at last. The city of gold is spread out before us. In the
foreground valley, the parched stones of a graveyard fight
with clumps of grass and shrubs for space. I am bored with
camel rides and panoramas, so my attention is easily caught
by a dozen or so people, slowly moving below me through
the valley in the distance. They are dressed in black and
carry what looks like a tabletop with something on it, cov-
ered by cloth. As I look closely, I realize that the object on
the table is a lifeless human body and I am watching a
funeral.

"Where is the coffin?" I asked, turning to my Israeli friend.
"In the holy city," he replies, "there are no coffins. The earth
herself is the box. Watch what happens now." The mourners gather around the freshly dug grave. We are much too
far away to hear, but I presume there are, as we rabbis say,
"some words," and then, while the tabletop is set at the
edge of the grave, a member of the *ḥevrah kaddisha* actually climbs down into the pit. The cords which hold the
corpse to the board are now loosened, the board is carefully
teeter-tottered halfway over the foot of the grave, and as
those on top slowly continue to raise their end, the man in
the grave slides his hands under the shoulders of the body
and gently guides it to its final resting place in the holy
earth. The member of the *ḥevrah* is helped up and out. The
grave is filled. The mourners form two lines. The camel ride
is over.

Some Personal Thoughts on Jewish Spirituality

Philip E. Miller

When the invitation first came for some personal thoughts on some aspect of Jewish spirituality, I demurred because I strongly believe that a person's spirituality is comparable to one's sexuality. That is, what one does in private does not necessarily mirror what one does in public, and while I tolerate what people do in public, I do not need to know or even want to know what another person does in private.

What changed my mind, however, was the reaction I received to the *devar Torah* I presented during the Wednesday morning service the week of Hanukkah. I will not recapitulate it here. Anyone who wishes a copy need only ask me. I do feel it is necessary, however, to introduce myself, for while many do know my name and what I do at the College–Institute, they do not know me as a person, and accordingly, do not know the background to my comments. Briefly summarized, I was born and raised in Providence, Rhode Island and received my primary Jewish education at two synagogues: Emanu-El, the major Conservative congregation, to which the entire family were members because the older generation were among its active founders during the 1920s, and Beth-El, the major Reform Congregation, to which my parents were spiritually and intellectually drawn. Beth-El's scholarly rabbi, William G. Braude, was a friend of each of my parents separately even before they had met. My father was a member of Rabbi Braude's celebrated Humash study circle, and my mother studied Hebrew with Rabbi Braude when she was an undergraduate at Brown University's Pembroke College. If I had a spiritual exemplar in my youth, it certainly was Rabbi Braude, and while I have had my own spiritual odyssey over the past thirty years, I find myself, in middle age, returning to the ideas Rabbi Braude represented.

For my undergraduate studies I attended the Institute of Language and Literatures at Georgetown University. This was at a time when there were many persons of color on campus, but they were largely embassy brats; as for Afro-Americans, one could count the number on one hand and have fingers left over. The basketball team was lily-white and Irish. The spirit of Vatican Two had yet to be enunciated, and "theologically motivated" anti-Semitism was pervasive. Moreover, I discovered purely by accident that there may have been a quota on the number of Jewish undergraduates at that time. I stayed because I wanted the education I felt only the Institute could offer. Besides, DC was a wonderful and exciting place to be an undergraduate during the mid-1960s.

As an antidote to Georgetown, I took advantage of an opportunity during my freshman year (the spring of 1964) to spend ten weeks in Israel. Eights weeks were to be spent working on a kibbutz, with fourteen days of touring scattered throughout the summer. I could easily write a book about my experiences that summer, for Israel was a very different place before the '67 War. The society was still very ideological, very socialist. Few people my age spoke any English; their parents all spoke perfect English as a result of the Mandate, but they bore a hatred for the British, and by extension, for the language, which they often pretended not to know. People of culture spoke French—few graduate students went to the United States; France was the country of choice. If only for self-preservation, I had to learn Hebrew!

As a result of that experience I developed a passion for the Hebrew language, which I spent every free moment studying. And because Hebrew was not regularly taught at the Institute, and Arabic was, Arabic eventually became my declared minor. In spite of a rigorous curriculum, I took a part-time job in order to save money for a return trip to Israel the summer of 1965. That summer of 1965 was even more intense in terms of personal experiences.

Rather than get bogged down, let me fast forward over the following details: I was graduated from Georgetown on

June 5, 1967, the very day the Six Day War began. Three months later I began graduate school at the University of Michigan in Near Eastern Studies. It was at a time during which The New Left's political activity was at its height; even then Ann Arbor was a hot bed of anti-Israel and pro-Arab sentiment. Being an Arabic major might appear to have put me at a disadvantage, but the opposite was actually true. I developed some very close relationships with Arab colleagues because the Department of Near Eastern Languages and Literatures was under the near-dictatorial control of its chairman, George Cameron, who, although not personally disposed toward Israel, never allowed politics to intrude into the Department's daily life. (After he retired in 1969 things became very polarized as an Arab-American who did not share Cameron's neutrality succeeded him. Cameron, by the way, has a very special place in my heart, for one of the last things he did before retiring was appoint me Teaching Fellow in Arabic, which saved me from the draft and Vietnam.)

Socially, my circle of personal friends in Ann Arbor were strongly Zionist, with many being religiously Orthodox. I had many acquaintances in the Orthodox crowd, and so found myself attending services fairly regularly. But these Orthodox friends never tried to get me to become one of them and I never sought to enter their inner circle. But I did learn a good deal about liturgy and to appreciate what they called "good davening." How I left my first dissertation (in Arabic linguistics) uncompleted and turned to library science as a career is another story. Suffice it to say that I came to Hebrew Union College–Jewish Institute of Religion on July 1, 1973.

So where am I now? In order to make a statement about my own spirituality, I must draw on the analogy of a piece of iron between the poles of two magnets. At times I am drawn to one, and at times to another. One magnet attracting me is that three- thousand-year continuum we call Judaism. As a student of Judaism in all its historical manifestations, I am drawn to its every aspect and nuance. The interplay of tradition and innovation plays an important role within the continuum, and within this interplay the pivotal role of halakhah cannot be ignored. The second magnet attracting me is our present context: American society at the end of the twentieth century. And part and parcel of both magnets is the nearly two-hundred-year tradition which comprises Reform Judaism. It is a tension in my life which is visible to those who know me.

Yet aside from the tension between the two poles, I find myself in a position of added insight which persons wholly drawn to one side or than other may not be able to perceive. Let me give you two examples which bear an interesting resemblance: Rabbi Geoffrey Goldberg once told me a story which he had heard from Rabbi Ignaz Maybaum, a teacher of his at Leo Baeck College, who in turn probably heard it from his uncle, Rabbi Sigmund Maybaum. The philosopher Hermann Cohen is alleged to have said that tears came to his eyes when he recited *Kiddush,* while an Orthodox Jew, in response, said that he said *Kiddush* to be "*yotse*" (fulfill a religious obligation). For that Orthodox Jew, the

halakhic obligation to sanctify the day was the linchpin of
his spirituality, whilst for Cohen, perhaps in disregard of the
halakhic aspect, the emotional reaction grounded his per-
ception of the spiritual. Both were right, and neither was
wrong, in a sense. But the Orthodox Jew missed out on
holiness, as defined by Rudolf Otto, while Cohen was perhaps attracted only by this kind of holiness, and missed out
on an important aspect of Jewish culture.

The second story, somewhat similar, but clearly different,
is something that happened at the Hillel House in Ann
Arbor in 1971 or so. Some friends and I were sitting in a
lounge at the Hillel House engaged in a general bull session. The Hillel's rabbi joined us—he himself was in his
mid-twenties, so he did fit in as "one of us." This rabbi was
Orthodox, of the modern variety, down to his "*kippah seru-
gah,*" and he was a chain-smoker whose head was always
wreathed in blue-gray smoke. A *ba'al teshuvah* type came
over and joined the conversation. At one point the BT said,
"Rabbi, can you help me? I *daven,* I say *Tehillim,* but nothing happens. As hard as I try, I just can't connect when I
pray. Am I doing something wrong?" We waited for the
rabbi's answer. He sat there puffing on his cigarette and
finally looked up and replied through a cloud of smoke,
"Let me see if I understand. You expect to have an orgasm
every time you say Sh'ma Yisrael." (There is no way to rep-
licate his facetious rising Yiddish intonation.) We all sat
there stunned. On the face of it, his reply was crude, rude,
insensitive, patronizing, and a host of other derogatories,
but as I thought of it later, the impact of his answer was akin

to a Zen master's giving his disciple a koan, for his answer and a koan had something in common: that the absurdity is the reality.

What, on the surface, did the *ba'al teshuvah* expect from his praying? On the one hand, perhaps this Orthodox rabbi viewed praying as something obligatory from a halakhic point of view. The *ba'al teshuvah* was, after all, seeking to be Orthodox. What more did he want or need? Yet the rabbi knew that he was seeking something deeper, something experiential in his prayer, but he, in his crude way, was trying to let the *ba'al teshuvah* know that ecstasy in prayer is not necessarily an every day occurrence. Or perhaps even to be attempted.

Aside from having come to the College-Institute in 1973, you should also know that I have been an active longtime member of two Reform congregations: Temple Sholom of West Essex (Cedar Grove, NJ) and until recently Temple Rodeph Torah (Marlboro, NJ). I also served four years on the board of the latter. So I feel very much part of the mainstream of Reform Judaism, yet because of my own background, I sense that spiritual tension in my own life that makes me different from the mainstream Reform Jew, but I have not told you how it plays out.

After giving it much thought, I have determined that I am something of a Classical Reform Jew. Classical Reform Judaism possesses within it a profoundly spiritual dimension which is well exemplified in its worship practices, minimalist and deracinated as they might be. Above I invoked the name of Rudolf Otto, a Protestant theologian and historian of religion, whose seminal work, *The Idea of the Holy,* I feel still has much to teach us. For Otto, what is holy is not identical with beauty, morality, or even truth. Rather, holiness is experiential, inspired by majesty and awe.

For me, the ideal worship service bears a sense of majesty: the language of prayer—in Hebrew or English—aspires to poetry, and is not a contemporary dialogue in which the Almighty and the worshipper are engaged in a quiet tête-à-tête conversation. The music inspires grandeur. (I personally like choirs and an organ.) Perhaps I am behind the times, but I find guitars and/or Arab drums leave me cold. I also have a genuine aversion to syncopation in synagogue music, not to say clapping hands. And no, I do not like the pseudo-/quasi-/neo-Israeli music I find too often in many compositions played in our sanctuaries, for some of them remind me of bad movie or cabaret music.

When I consider much of the "new" synagogue music that so many find "moving," or "spiritual," the words of George Eliot come to mind:

> "It is a form of melody which expresses a puerile state of culture—a dangling, canting, see-saw kind of stuff—the passion and thought of people without any breadth of horizon. There is a sort of self-satisfied folly about every phrase of such melody: no cries of deep, mysterious passion, no conflict—no sense of the universal. . . . "

(George Eliot, *Daniel Deronda*)

Some people have accused me of elitism. What that means, I really am not sure. For myself, it is not a question of being elitist, for I do not think of myself as such. Rather, I think of it as a matter of taste. In short, Lewandowski's music still gives me a frisson; Debbie Friedman's gives me a headache. For me, Classical Reform Judaism best exemplifies Otto's notion of the holy.

I also want the person speaking from the pulpit, be it a rabbi, cantor, or a lay person, to teach me Torah, not to ignore the weekly Pentateuchal lection or use it as a springboard to discuss one's personal views of politics (domestic or foreign), give a book or movie review, or a pep talk on feeling good, or any of the other "contemporary" topics which are the subject of too many sermons. (I also feel too many, rabbis especially, use their pulpits to afflict us with their own Op-Ed pieces, which the *New York Times* could never consider publishing.)

When I attend many contemporary Reform services, I feel like I am at a *kumsitz* or a campfire, except I am not seeking that kind of camaraderie. In every respect, I want the service I attend to be an aesthetic experience, both verbally and musically. Now I clearly recognize that "aestheticism in worship" can also lead to the attitude that says, "I can pray anywhere: the woods, in the mountains, by the sea; wherever I encounter God." Very true, and I even admit to praying in the woods, mountains, and by seashores. But I do not make a practice of it, for I feel that it is not especially Jewish. *"Al tifrosh min ha-tsibur"* is the admonition in our tradition—I feel I must pray in and with a community.

Unfortunately I find the community with which I enjoy praying seems to be shrinking. Too many of our leaders,

both religious and lay, have bought in to the view that
prayer is a celebration of community. We all stand around
and sing our own praises, albeit in the name of God: "How
wonderful we are that we have gathered to praise God!"
And we Jews are not alone. In the Christian world, especially amongst Roman Catholics, worship has turned into a
self-centered love-fest. Catholic traditionalists point out that
Roman Catholic worship started to go down the drain when
the centrality of worship was no longer the Mystery of the
Mass, but the celebration of the community. I see the same
thing happening around us: We have in our worship
stopped celebrating the centrality of the holy, of Shabbat
and *Yamim Tovim* in favor of celebrating ourselves. Plainly
out, too many of our religious leaders have confounded the
narcissistic celebration of community with the quest for holiness.

One aspect of our collective worship here at the College–
Institute that puzzles me is (for so many) the newly learned
"physicality." I really have nothing against "shokkeling," but
I ask: How and why do people who never "shokkeled"
before do so now? What was it about that one year experience in Israel that has turned so many into latter-day bob-
bing ducks? I confess to having tried shokkeling myself, and
all I got out of it was sense of nausea and dizziness, something akin to seasickness. I have gone to the trouble of asking some of the shokkelers why they do it, and the
invariable answer is "to intensify the sense of prayer."

All this has led me to speculate that perhaps some of
these persons are trying to pray with "*kavvanah*." Or per-

haps they think it will help them attain God's presence. Thinking on it some more, I found myself wondering if it was not possible that for some, these physical externals are actually a sign of something else. By that I mean, perhaps there are individuals who have come to the College–Institute out of deep spiritual motivation, and knowing that spirituality is a hot topic, feel they have to do something to demonstrate that they are attempting "to find God" or to develop their own "*spirituality*." But they feel they do not have the proper intellectual background or grounding in texts, so they "*shokkel*," giving an explicit sign to those they wish to impress. Does "shokkeling" give them a sense of "the holy" in Otto's sense? I truly hope so. But I also hope it is not self delusion brought on by the heightened sense of ethnicity that a year spent in Israel can give one.

Yet in the Jewish quest for holiness a special aspect has been its hallmark, for which we have textual testimony as far back as *Tanna'im* in the *Midrash Halakhah,* namely the intensive study of Scripture and related literature. I would contend that this aspect is unique to Judaism among the three monotheistic faiths. While Christianity and Islam do possess "sacraments" and "holy obligation" as their means for finding holiness, we, with perhaps the exception of the Buddhists, are unique in our making the study of our sacred literature a supreme act of holiness. Indeed, Buddhists use the term "Dharma" in its broadest sense in a manner very similar to the Jewish use of "Torah." But Buddhism does not have the imperative, *"asher kiddeshanu be-mitsvotav ve-tsivanu la-'asok be-divrey Torah."*

While it is possible to explore spirituality without the textual tradition, the results will, in my opinion, perforce be shallow in terms of what is authentically Jewish. Judaism has traditionally been a religious system in which one first mastered texts and then applied these texts to one's experiences. What I fear is a generation of Jewish leaders who, because they do not have such a textual foundation, will claim to have found "Jewish spirituality" in their own personal feelings. "Le-mah ha-davar domeh?" I now recall a conversation I had over twenty years ago with Rabbi A. Stanley Dreyfus grimacing as he said, "Creative service too often signals a rabbi's ignorance of the text of the liturgy."

I fear, therefore, for students who come to the College–Institute and who feel they can explore their inner holiness without immersing themselves in the textual tradition, for they are squandering the most valuable opportunity they have for developing the richest source for their own spirituality. Aside from worship and the performance of mitsvot, the principal source of Jewish spirituality has for nearly two millennia come from an engagement with our holy sacred literature. To quote from my *devar Torah*:

> . . . how wonderful it is to experience that amazing moment of insight when not only the words of midrash explicate the words of Torah, but when the words of Torah illuminate the words of midrash! In such moments of insight, such as I had [during the preparation of this *devar Torah*], I cannot help but feel profoundly blessed. It is my prayer that it be the lot of each and every one of us to encounter such blessing time and again as we study our ancient textual tradition.

. . . [Yet] so many of us are concerned about our personal relationship to God, and one can see this in the intensity of praying of some in this synagogue. But in my opinion, too many of us are putting too much stock in what are ultimately superficialities. My unsolicited advice is to leave God alone to get on with the daily work of renewing Creation. Our personal relationship to God? Don't worry about it. Believe me, it is something that happens over time, one cannot take a pill for it and gain instant knowledge; it is something that does take care of itself. To invoke Bialik: *Im yesh le'nafshekha la-da'at. . . .* If we want to know the source of Israel's greatness, let us go to the *bet ha-midrash!* Let us spend as much time as we can with our sacred texts, in Hebrew, in English, in any language we understand—for they truly have been the profoundest source of spirituality for our people for more than two thousand years.

Postscript by Philip E. Miller

A year ago I wrote an essay on Jewish spirituality which I felt mirrored the state of my own personal belief. Mark Twain once gave a useful piece of advice, that if one has a good idea, one should write it down, stick it in a drawer, and not look at it again for two weeks; if after that time one feels the idea is still good, then one should proceed with it. For better or worse, the ideas I wrote down did not sit in a drawer, but were published. And now, after a year's reflection, I wonder if, had I heeded Twain's advice, I would have gone ahead and seen my thoughts put into print. It is not that I no longer agree with what I wrote. I am certainly not repudiating what I wrote at that time, but I am not certain that it fully reflected what I thought I meant. Or at least how I feel now.

Like any of us, I am a product of my times. And regardless of how I think I may be able to overcome individual limitations and circumstances, I remain in many ways reflective of my environment. I say this, for after decades of experimentation, I find myself having gone full cycle, returning to that form of Judaism in which I was reared. Referred to by many as Classical Reform, and rather out of favor within much or our movement, yet I feel I owe no one an explanation, let alone a defense of it. Granted, there may be fewer and fewer Reform Jews who are spiritually satisfied with that worship experience they label as "sterile." I, for one, am still very comfortable with it and would not change it for the world.

So what is it exactly that I want to say now that I did not last year? There are several individual points I would like to make.

1. Last year I took a view that some felt was inflexible, namely, that the only path to spirituality, Jewishly speaking, was via close engagement with our sacred literature. Such an approach, however much I find this applicable to myself and desirable for others, would, I admit, be hubris to universalize.

2. I feel I must say that I, as a Reform Jew, find myself wondering what "Judaism" is. It is, on the one hand, what our tradition teaches us to think, act, and do, and yet, on the other, it is ultimately what people who call themselves Jews do. The halakhah may offer a universal framework, but in

the end there is much variation within it, such that I see the societal and individual differences as ultimately creating "Judaisms."

Let me try to give concrete examples. I knew of a gentleman who only ate kosher food, both within his home and without, and who attended Sabbath morning services every week at an Orthodox synagogue. Yet on his way home from the synagogue, he would always stop at the newsstand and buy a copy of the Saturday edition of the *Forward,* which he read cover to cover that afternoon, while listening to the live radio broadcast of the Metropolitan Opera. This individual was comfortable with his own personal practice, yet someone more "observant" might find fault with him. Wherein lies the problem? With the individual in question, or with his more "observant" coreligionist?

In the past, it has been Judaism writ large that has decided who was observant and who was not. While this perhaps was one of those factors that helped Judaism survive millennia, I, on the other hand, would submit that the individual was happy in his way of life and otherwise undisturbed by what others saw as contractions or inconsistencies. I, as a Reform Jew, would ask: Who has the problem with whom? Perhaps the problem ought to lie not with the individual but with the one who was finding fault.

To change the subject for just a moment, but returning to it immediately, I am known as a student of Karaism, the sect originating in the Middle Ages that rejected the authority of the Talmud and of the rabbis. I once took part in a discussion at a conference in which we were asked how and why

Karaism failed to capture and hearts and minds of vast num-
bers of Jews and thus pose a serious threat to rabbinic Judaism. (This may appear contrary to the image projected in
geonic literature, but in my view, the Karaites were never a
threat on a large scale, but served as a convenient bogey-
man for the rabbis to assert their authority.) Karaism prided
itself on its loyalty to the letter of Scripture, while the Talmud was essentially a record of how the rabbis accommo-
dated popular practice to the spirit of the law. Moreover,
early Karaism appears to have been ascetic as well as Pales-
tino-centric, while the majority of Jews lived far from Palestine and were not interested in austerity for its own sake. In
short, Karaism, in its idealism, sealed its own fate and
doomed itself to failure.

To return to the matter at hand, I see modern Orthodox
Judaism, which portrays itself as the staunch defender of tradition and enforcer of talmudic truth, as the betrayer of
both. Reform Judaism, on the other hand, is more realistic
about what people do in their individual lives, especially in
this postmodern (postsecular?) world. To claim, as Orthodox
Judaism does, that the truth lies in tradition is to falsify history, for the Judaism of the gaonim in Babylonia was hardly
that of Moslem Spain in the thirteenth century or of Boro
Park in the twentieth.

3. In matters of flexibility and accommodation, I feel that
Reform Judaism offers a position which is historically more
accurate. All human societies are syncretistic; none is
"pure." Similarly, no religion is immune from external influence. Somewhere along the line new practices are intro-

duced (or "born"), and old ones are modified, even dropped. Someone in 1996 may experiment with techniques of Tibetan Buddhist visualization, and by 2096 it may become "normative" Judaism. Does this seem too bizarre? Approximately thirteen hundred years ago, Jews in Sassanian Babylonia took oaths on the names of Zoroastrian angels and used a typical Zoroastrian formula to annul such vows; the gaonim, powerless to curtail a practice they condemned, finally co-opted it into the liturgy for Yom Kippur as *Kol Nidrei!* Similarly, some one thousand years ago the institution of *Yortsayt* was unknown, as was the liturgical institution of *Yizkor,* let alone memorial candles. Yet some innovative individual in Ashkenaz mimicked what Christian neighbors were doing, and new Jewish practices were created which are the height of "traditional" Judaism today.

4. As there can be and are Judaisms today, so too are there paths to God. And the "High Textual" position I espoused last year must be seen as only one, but not *the* only one. While it may have enjoyed a preeminence in the past, it cannot preclude others today (even if they are not my personal cup of tea). I may not fancy a Lakota sweat lodge for a religious experience, but I would not preclude anyone else's exploring it as a possibility for spiritual enrichment. In short, I feel that Judaism in general and Reform Judaism in particular must not shy away from them because they are new or foreign.

There may be those who would brand experimentation or syncretism as *darkhei ha-emori,* that is, "the ways of the Amorites," the term used in rabbinic literature to designate

superstitious heathen practices not otherwise explicitly pro-
hibited in the Torah (see Lev. 18:3). And while the admonition may serve to scare away some, it does ultimately beg
the issue.

Let me conclude this point by reiterating: while such
experimentation may not appeal to me personally, far be it
from me to find fault or to condemn it.

5. Reform Judaism has always prided itself on its critical
attitude. But lately I find a distinct lack of critical judgment
when it comes to the mindset of many Reform Jews. Lest I
be misunderstood, I am not critical of piety, for piety, that
genuinely worshipful frame of mind, is a virtue. Rather, I am
critical of pietism, the excessive expression of uncritical,
exaggerated, even mindless piety—especially when in the
name of spirituality. In all religions the pious person tends
to be humble and compassionate, gaining wisdom over
time, while the pietists tends to be arrogant, becoming intol-
erant over time. Let us eschew pietism!

6. Another problem area today is our own personal iden-
tity as Reform Jews. On the one hand, I resent the "Israeliza-
tion" taking place in North American Reform Judaism. Israel,
as a secular Jewish state, I feel, has nothing to offer our personal beliefs and practice. I even go so far as to resent the
claim that Israel gives us a "sense of pride." Indeed, I feel
that our Reform Judaism has much it can teach the secular
Jewish state, especially in the application of social action, in
the spheres of civil and human rights, within her own bor-
ders. This is especially needed since the so-called "religious"
element in Israel has been remiss in allowing a dangerous

mentality to take hold, especially among the young. Dare I call it how I perceive it? *Blut und Boden*. And I find this especially frightening and ultimately detrimental, if not destructive, of Judaism at large in the long run. (The assassination of Prime Minister Rabin was hardly an isolated affair. A number of years ago, similarly religiously motivated young men planted bombs in a calculated campaign of terror which killed and maimed major Arab mayors in West Bank towns. The guilty were brought to justice, but no attempt was made within the so-called "religious" community to curb such parochial fanaticism. It was only when Jewish blood was shed, and when the international community sat up and took notice, that these "religious" people took steps to distance themselves from these individuals they otherwise nurtured.)

7. Finally, I, a Classical Reform Jew, one who cherishes the High Textual Tradition, realize that mine is a path that does not appeal to many. Yet I must let the many know that as I appreciate—and even endorse—their spiritual quest, I demand my right as a Reform Jew, whose beliefs and practices come our of our historical experience, to remain a Classical Reform Jew and to practice Judaism as I see fit. I intend to continue to attend the synagogue with a bare head, and this undoubtedly may offend some, and my explicit lack of enthusiasm for certain new modes of worship may not please others. But we must in the end realize, however, that as Reform Jews, we are all legitimate. Our strength is in our diversity.

Jewish Spirituality:
The Way of Love

Carol Ochs

S pirituality is not theology or history or liturgy or rabbinic codes. Spirituality is our relationship to God, with all its ups and downs, engagements and withdrawals. To deepen and strengthen this relationship, we make use of the insights we gain through our theology and through our understanding of Jewish history. When we want to be in communication with God, we use our established forms of liturgy and look to the guidance of our codes. But all of these are only the instruments we use in our quest to develop our relationship. We may build a house, but it remains only a structure and does not become a home without the love of the people who reside there. We can discover something, but it becomes a treasure only when we value it. And we can structure a relationship with God, but it becomes fruitful only when we imbue it with our love.

Most Jewish prayers are written in the plural, but our love for God must be an individual experience. When we enter into marriage, the words we use to describe our relationship have been formed by the community. Our expectations for marriage are socially constructed. The marriage ceremony is codified by our faith. And yet, when we go home, close the door, and begin our day-to-day lives, the actual relationship with our spouse is individual and deeply personal. Our relationship to God is no less formed by the stories that have shaped our faith, described our history, and given form to our experiences. But while much of our relationship is expressed communally, it remains essentially individual and personal.

The love between each individual Jew and God is lived out day by day in all our tasks, our conversations, our tears, and our celebrations, but, finally, we don't infer the love, we experience it with all its joy, liberation, and healing. Before that can happen, God must represent more for us than an ethical standard, a first principle, a God of our forebears. Somehow God must become our personal God, with all the intensity such a relationship may entail. This can be a scary prospect, one we are not always sure we want.

Many commonly held notions about spirituality are not true of Jewish spirituality. Jewish spirituality is not other-worldly. As children, we learn concepts by separation and distinction, so the "holy" is first perceived in contrast with the secular. But in a fully formed spirituality, the holy is found in and through all that we experience. Loving God does not mean turning to some point outside the world: we discover God only by turning to life. As a people, we may already have discovered the holy within the daily rounds of our lives. But individually, we may need to set apart some time and space to enable us to reconnect with the freshness and power our ancestors experienced when they discovered that the holy resides in and through all of their lives.

Western writings on spirituality have emphasized the solitary route to salvation—going off alone into the desert. Jewish spirituality gives far more weight to the communal aspect of our lives. We are, thankfully, aware of how much we owe both to our tradition and to our community, which lifts us up when we falter in our ongoing conversation with God. Jewish spirituality also shows us how central our human loves are for enabling us to grow in our love of God. We must recognize the role of community and must also reflect on our individual contribution; this requires knowing ourselves and striving to become free of all that obstructs our openness.

Many writings on spirituality have dwelt on the journey as th most potent model for imaging the spiritual life. Indeed, the journey image originates in our Exodus from Egypt; but Jewish spirituality has always understood the journey in conjunction with the images of relatedness and love. This love is present throughout the *Tanakh,* but is nowhere represented better than in the Song of Songs, which Rabbi Akiva deemed the holiest scriptural book.

Our love of God brings us ever more deeply into the world. We can love God in and through everything we know in this world. We learn to experience everything in this world in its relationship to God, and so come to know the world in all its mystery and awesomeness. The most important things we know can be fully known only through loving. Knowledge that grows out of our love of God teaches us that there are aspects of reality that we cannot know until we love. How shyly the person we love opens up to us over years of loving, and the wonder and mystery of the other does not dissipate after a lifetime. With equal modesty and diffidence, a scene opens up to us, a piece of music reveals its depths. Ernest Becker expresses his awareness of the mystery and magnificence of reality:

> The great boon of repression is that it makes it possible to live decisively in an overwhelmingly miraculous and incomprehensible world, a world so full of beauty, majesty, and terror that if animals perceived it all they would be paralyzed to act.[1]

And yet in the face of this awe and wonder we can, remarkably, respond not with terror but with love, not with fear but with trust. Learning to love God demands all of ourselves. Love is something we feel, but more than that, it is the shape we give to our lives. We know that parents' love for their children is much more than having warm tender

---

1. Ernest Becker, *The Denial of Death* (New York: Free Press, 1973), p. 50.

feelings. Parental love stretches the parents and takes them into worlds they could have not imagined. "Go forth from your native land and from your father's house to the land that I will show you," is the call to all parents. Everything that we love pulls us. Each child is our favored child, the one we love, and with each child we must radically let go. Love never leaves us unchanged. Spirituality, which is a way of loving and therefore a way of knowing and being, is at its deepest core a way of becoming transformed. We are not yet who we are fully meant to be. Only through loving God and becoming open to God's transformative love can we hope to be shaped more nearly to our ideal self.

Spirituality is also life's only enduring adventure. Ecclesiastes shows us the vanity in most attempts at human fulfillment: progress, human wisdom, pleasure of the senses, power, wealth. The only goal that can motivate us for a lifetime is a deepening love of God. William Blake wrote:

And we are put on earth a little space,
That we may learn to bear the beams of love.[2]

The span of human life feels very short when we recognize how much we have to learn. First we must learn that we are loved. That sounds easy, but most of us do not believe that we are lovable. We feel as if we must do something to merit the love that has brought us into being and sustained us. But love has nothing to do with our merit but

---

2. William Blake, "Songs of Innocence," in *Selected Poetry and Prose,* ed. Northrup Frye (New York: Random house, 1953), p. 25.

with God's grace. Love is not a salary, but a gift. Once we allow ourselves to recognize, be open to, and accept that love, once we can bear the beams of love that are given to us, then we can express the love that is within us. We become part of the circle of love that begins with God and returns to God but in between encompasses all of creation. And all along we are uncovering the love that is apparent in everything to which we fully attend. Each *berakhah* marks a moment, an opportunity, to uncover the love that rests in all that surrounds and supports us.

But even though loving God is what gives meaning to our lives, we hold back. We fear that letting God into our lives will overwhelm us and bring on upheaval and disruption. We fear the images that fill the *Tanakh* of those who love God and then are tested in frightening ways. We fear loss of control. We need to be reassured that God speaks to each of us in the native language of our soul. And indeed, God spoke one way to Abraham, another way to Rebecca, and a third way to Job. We cannot, of course, live a life appropriate for someone else. Our lives belong to us in such an intimate way that we cannot really imagine being and feeling like another person. God created us in our uniqueness and therefore, we must conclude, values our uniqueness, so loving God will not turn us into someone else but will help us become fully who we most essentially are. Spirituality can give some discipline and shape to our fear and fascination. All great loves require discipline, constancy, and faithfulness. Love is the great lodestone pulling us out of our constricted selves into the fullness of life.

On Yom Kippur evening, as we enter into the awesome time of taking stock and reciting the Confession, we remember all the many ways we have been educated to love and relate to God:

We are Your people, and You are our God.
We are Your children, and You are our Parent.

This prayer reminds us that we must learn what it is to love as a child, as a spouse, and as a parent if we are to aspire to the love that contains them all. We learn about the complexities of all these forms of love by living in this world and by living in the world of the *Tanakh*. We are educated about the difficulties of family relationships through the rivalries described in Genesis. We learn about the love of spouse in the Song of Songs and the compassion of parent to child that God expresses in Jeremiah:

Truly, Ephraim is a dear son to Me,
A child that is dandled!
Whenever I have turned against him,
My thoughts would dwell on him still.
That is why My heart yearns for him;
I will receive him back in love,
declares the Lord.

(Jer. 31:20)

We are repeatedly shown how to love, how to forgive, how to have compassion: through Hosea's forgiving his wife, through Malachi's prophecy that parents and their children will be reconciled. All of our texts and all of our experiences are meant to educate us to the realization that "an eternal love have I conceived for you" (Jer. 31:3), to which we hope at last to grow to the point where we can respond, "And thou shalt love the Lord thy God with all thy heart, with all thy soul, and with all thy might" (Deut. 6:5). We learn to love in all the ways God teaches us.

This universal openness to God is shared by many Western and Eastern spiritualities. We cannot, however, appropriate a world unmediated by language, and Jewish spirituality is uniquely mediated through the native language of our souls, Judaism. Things can become real to us only when they take on form, and language is the primary form through which we can begin to understand the many chaotic phenomena that surround us. Through language we discover that someone else has experienced the same thing we have; the existence of a name affirms that someone else has traveled this route. The essential texts of Judaism give us a way to name, reflect upon, and understand our experiences.

When the Children of Israel made an idol of the Golden Calf, they needed some concrete, tangible image to sustain them in Moses' absence. Being so new to freedom, the Israelites experienced Moses' absence as abandonment. They lacked the vocabulary to remember the miracles that had brought them so far. Instead, they could grasp only their own terror. Memory works best when things and events have names that are fitting and powerful.

Unlike the Children of Israel, who had no such precedent or memory, we have the story of the Exodus to help us recognize and name our own miracles. The text, which is the story of our people, becomes a map for understanding our own lives. And our lives, in turn, become the tools whereby the story of our people becomes intelligible to us. The two texts, Torah and our lives, are inextricably intertwined. The story did not happen once upon a time, a long time ago, and all we have had since then are leftovers. It happened, it continues to happen, and it will continue to happen for all of time. God renews the work of creation constantly, and we experience this renewal. We are forever being led out of slavery, and we personally face the hardships of the wilderness and the illumination at Sinai. Each of us, in our own life, must become part of the covenant.

As we turn to the *Tanakh,* we remember that biblical texts were never written primarily for academic study. Their first use was to illuminate and transform our lives. To properly understand them, then, we need to bring the texts to our lives and our lives to the texts. Love is very difficult; it is probably the source of most of life's joy but also its pain. We do not know what to love or how to love. But this is precisely what the *Tanakh* aims to teach us.

Ezekiel had a vision of wheels within wheels. For all their interconnected complexity, these wheels were able to move in any direction and did not veer when they moved. Our own motion is far more erratic: we orbit around our egos, wills, and desires. Using a related analogy, we can say that we are like the earth turning on the axis of human existence while orbiting around the sun, which is God's existence. We are free to turn on our axis and get caught up in the concerns of this world as long as our orbit still centers on God. But when we try to go in the many different directions required to meet the needs of our egos, wills, and desires, then our experience is one of divergence and frustration. Only when we turn again to be centered on God do we experience once more the easeful motion of Ezekiel's wheels. At last the erratic motion becomes smoothed out as Judaism offers us the central principle that can unite our head, heart, and soul. Or, as Dante writes at the end of the *Paradiso,* "But now my desire and will, like a wheel that spins with even motion, were revolved by the Love that moves the sun and the other stars."[3]

There can be no Jewish spirituality without Jewish scholarship. But the scholarship finds its fullest employment in fostering the relationship between each of us, all of us, and God. So while we build our houses of faith, join in our communities of worship, and live by our codes of law, it is love that makes all these the outer garments covering a deeply inhabited faith.

3. Dante Alighieri, *Paradiso,* canto XXXIII, line 40, trans. John D. Sinclair (New York: Oxford University Press, 1939).

Toward a Personal Definition of Jewish Spirituality

Kerry Olitzky

T here seems to be a variety of acceptable definitions for spirituality and a plethora of programs which are intended to be spiritual in nature. While a definition of spirituality might seem to elude many among us, such a definition seems rather straightforward to me. Spirituality is the process through which the individual strives to meet God. It is more than a surrender to unconditional faith, and much more than just the establishment of a sense of community—however indispensable both may be to the securing of a Jewish self and a Jewish future. Spirituality may be the current buzz word that is in vogue in many of our congregations and communities, but the struggle for personal meaning in the context of a growing relationship with the Almighty is not new to the Jewish religious community. Perhaps it is only the vocabulary of Jewish renewal that makes it seem new. Since this is, for some, a somewhat foreign vocabulary—often borrowed from other faith communities—many of us may find it difficult to call it our own. Nevertheless, I am committed to the spiritual struggle because I know that it can sweep the individual heavenward. I've tasted the messianic. I've danced with the ministering angels. I know that such a level of religious ecstasy is possible for me: a liberal and nonmystic. As a result, I want to return to that place often—and bring others along with me. For me, the joy really is in the journey.

For countless generations, people have been faced with a spiritual hunger or even emptiness. This yearning to reach beyond the self is not new. Perhaps we feel it more poignantly today because we have acknowledged the fact that the modern age—the age of self—has failed and we are ready to go beyond it. And we finally have acknowledged the increasing number in our midst who have tried to fill that spiritual hunger through alcohol or drugs or gambling or sex or food, as well as those who have totally despaired and taken their own lives. These are not the ways to reach God or fill the void that many among us may feel. Yet we realize that a sense of the spiritual can be accomplished through a variety of methods. Admittedly, while not my personal preference, even the *mitnagged* approach to Judaism is a form of spirituality, especially when it is transformed as rationalism for the Reform Jew or even as the unyielding intellectualism of the scholar. To be sure, the musar of the *mitnagged* must also be included in such a discussion on spirituality.

However, for me, the study of sacred text accompanied by both a routine (*keva*) and spontaneous (*kavvanah*) out-pouring of prayer is the chief vehicle to reach a spiritual state. One must contextualize the other. I recognize that this sounds like the "company line," what a seminary faculty member might be expected to say. This is not a knee-jerk response. Rather it is personal testimony, the kind that emanates from the soul. It is what works for me. Of course, I understand that the way of the mystic seems much more exciting to the uninitiated than does the life of a scholar. As a result, study does not seem like the prime vehicle for reaching God. No matter how such study is approached, it seems flat and one-dimensional. For those attracted to mysticism, spirituality is not possible within the confines of the written word. Instead, it is only possible outside of the text, perhaps in nature. Such spirituality begins as a lonely vigil on the top of a mountain or at the shore of a majestic ocean or even by sitting quietly near a peaceful country lake. Meditation is usually part of this type of mystical process and often includes the repetition of a bit of sacred text, a *kavvanah,* what we might call a Jewish mantra. And in the end, when it works, there is a total abdication (or loss) of self in exchange for a complete union (*devekut*) with God. Thus, our sense of self becomes totally submerged in our knowledge of God.

While I resonate with this mystical process—often even yearn for it, trying bits of it on my own—it's not so easy for me. I am not a mystic. I do not feel capable of such mystical pursuits. I am only a rabbi, a teacher, trying to teach what I have learned from my teachers, who, in turn, taught me what they had been taught. So I turn to Torah, the spiritual touchstone of the Jewish people, for inspiration and insight, as a way of refracting my experiences with the world and learning from them. I focus on Torah because sacred text provides me with a prism to stare into my own soul. Moreover, Torah captures the divine light which allows me to see myself more clearly. When I place a mirror in front of the text, I see my own reflection in the lives of my ancestors. In such discernment, I am also able to find a personal way to respond to the ever-present sense of God that I feel in my life.

Whether we speak of the struggles of faith of our forebears or our own challenges of daily living, it makes no difference. Their experience and ours can become fused in our study. So I review the text regularly in order to keep my life in balance, to give me direction in a rudderless world. That's what *parashat ha-shavuah,* for example, is all about. I plumb its depths in order to gain mooring, to achieve a sense of stability in an otherwise rocky earthly existence. And as I consider its meaning, I do not look for others to provide me with answers—nor am I prepared to suggest solutions to others who are asking similar questions for their own lives. That would rob us both of the opportunity to struggle with the text and make it our own. The daily struggle of faith—rather than its easy resolution—is what makes such a spiritual journey essentially Jewish. People often think that faith should come to us easily, without a struggle, much like we seem to see in other faith communities. Yet Jewish belief does not work that way. Jewish faith does not come easy, nor should it. Such profound faith grows over time. We reach it in uneven stages. Little by little. We get there step by step. Not always in the same order, nor at the same pace. Maybe the rabbis were right: we really did have to go down and endure slavery in Egypt before we could be truly free in a land of promise. Perhaps this is what makes the trip all the more worthwhile.

Thus I enter the spiritual life of biblical characters, live with them as they confront their lives and grapple with their personal experiences with faith. When I pause in my study and take a moment to reflect on my own ongoing journey, I really believe that I have enriched the life of the text and, as a result, joined the path of Jewish history with my own. Through this process, I am bold enough to say that I have, in fact, enhanced the text. Through this process, my life becomes intertwined with those who have come before me. When I leave my study, I realize that as much as the text has left its imprint on me, I have also left my footprints along the path of my ancestors in the text and beyond. Our journeys through the Sinai and this desert we call life become fused. The sacred text is a spiritual legacy, documenting the relationship of individuals with God through history. Through study, I am able to join my struggle with theirs. In a way, as a result of our journey with our past, we all have the potential to become sacred texts. The study of Jewish text is therefore not merely an intellectual exercise. For some that is sufficient, but for me it is a place to meet God and in that encounter see the self more clearly—and be healed. In one way or another, we all need healing. Perhaps that is the ultimate goal of the spiritual journey.

A rabbi was once asked by his students, "What do you do before prayer?" Came the teacher's response, "I prepare for prayer." The students pressed their mentor and asked, "How do you prepare?" To this question, the rabbi replied, "I pray that I may be able to pray properly." How indeed does one ready oneself for such encounters with God? For me, the answer is self-evident. One reaches God through prayer. In the context of prayer—in a covenantal partnership with God—one searches out the potential to become transformed. Some will argue that study is a form of prayer, and I believe that the study of sacred text can indeed be a prayerful experience. It can even be said that prayer helps ready the individual for proper study.

For those among us who may grope for words of prayer, for the poetry which will communicate our exact emotions, traditional liturgy helps us to jump-start the process. With the images formed by those who have come before me, I am able to say what I want to say even before I am capable of saying it. But when my words of prayer are restrained by the liturgy and are not given expression through the liturgical process—instead falling prey to sacred drama or worse to the platitudes of a preacher—then even the familiar and generally comforting cadence of routine liturgy leaves me short and uninspired, unmotivated to reach beyond myself.

I believe in the power of prayer. Together with study, it forms my individual dialogue with God. That dialogue is an ongoing conversation. Established on the fiery mountain in the desert where we all began our journey, it is part of the covenant that I seek to maintain with God. I try to live a life reflective of that covenant, always conscious of that relationship with God. It is what helps me frame my life, all that I am and all that I do.

On reflection, it would seem that study and prayer should be sufficient for achieving the spiritual life. Perhaps for the rare ascetic such an approach is indeed enough. But such a posture does not seem to be the primary Jewish way. We need to interface with the world around us. It is part of who and what we are as human beings. Listen carefully to the advice of the rabbis when they instruct us to build our synagogues with windows of clear glass. By design, the rabbis are forcing us to maintain a perspective on the reality of the material world—beyond the walls of the *bet tefillah*—even while we are trying to gaze heavenward. This is particularly important for those of us who attempt to balance our liberal religious lives with feet firmly planted in contemporary society all around us, with all its vice and virtue. In this way, we can enter both the world of our grandparents and our grandchildren.

Moreover, ethical acts (such as those taught by various schools of musar) must guide our interaction with the world and shape our daily lives. They must indeed reflect what

Buber describes as that I-Thou relationship we are constantly trying to achieve. Shneur Zalman of Lyady seems to have something to say here. He retells the story when once he was studying upstairs in his son's home. On the floor below, his grandchild slept while his son studied nearby. The baby started crying, but the son—seated only a few feet away from the crib—was so involved with his study that he did not hear his own child crying. Distressed, Shneur Zalman descended the stairs, calmed the baby, then sternly addressed his son. He said, "You cannot reach the holy if you cannot hear the cry of a baby." In other words, it's not good to be so surrounded by holiness that the noise of the secular world does not disturb you. But always listen for the cry of a baby. Always! Shneur Zalman's lesson speaks directly to me. I see my work as an effort to constantly listen for that human cry—whether it emanates from the mouth of a baby or from a fellow Jew in distress.

And what about *mitzvot*? What role do these instructions for holiness play in our spiritual struggle? For me, *mitzvot* have a singular purpose. They help us to make sacred all that we do, all that we see, all that we are. In so doing, they help us in our endeavor to encounter God. *Mitzvot* are a path in themselves, a bridge between the secular and the sacred. As a Reform Jew, I am comfortable in acknowledging the fact that I do not feel addressed by all *mitzvot*. Yet I constantly consider them, one at a time, probing, analyzing, testing them. When I am ready, I bring them carefully and consciously into my religious life. As a result of this process, with those *mitzvot* which I have taken on, I am able to do so hearing the call from Sinai as an echo in my ears. And when I am fully immersed in any one *mitzvah,* I can hear the voice of God beckoning me to come closer. And so I do.

My Spiritual Journey

Lawrence W. Raphael

When I decided to write about my own personal spiritual life, I turned back to an ethical will I wrote almost two years ago. That will began as follows:

Dear Children: Matthew, Andrew, and Rachel,

It is February 25th, 1993 and I am writing an ethical will, a task which is usually completed before the High Holy Days. For a while I have been thinking of updating the one that I wrote ten years ago, and the recent events in our family's life have encouraged me to do so. When I wrote my first ethical will, you, Matthew, were 4 years old, Terrie was pregnant with Andrew, and Rachel was not even part of our vocabulary.

Now some twenty months later, I am rereading my ethical

will and note that I am continuing to think about all the relationships in my life and trying to establish some rhyme and reason in them. Each one of us is many things to others. In my case, I am the husband to Terrie and then the father to Matthew, Andrew, and Rachel. I was also the orphan son of my deceased mother Florence and my more recently-deceased father Joel, who died six months ago after a long decline in health following a stroke eight years ago.

In my immediate family I am also the brother of Marc and JoAnn. To other family, to close friends and to others, I constantly live in relationship. I continue to realize my existence as a husband first, then as a father, son, and brother, help clearly define who I am.

I wrote this version of my ethical will ten weeks after my mother died of a sudden heart attack. That event has greatly altered my thinking about so many things. I recall teaching a class session with the second-year rabbinic students just before my mother died. We were discussing funerals and I commented that it is very hard to know in advance how people are going to react to grief and sorrow. Little did I know that just a few days later I would be confronting the death of my mother.

I have found that nothing in my life prepared me for that event. No amount of rational thinking over my mother's declining health; no amount of thought about what should and could be done upon her death assisted me very much when the time came. I realize now that in spite of her long illness and the many times that she was close to death, I effectively denied that she would die.

Through trial and error I gradually learned what made sense in the process of mourning. I could not have anticipated what felt right during shiva, nor could I have anticipated the overwhelming need to say Kaddish daily during the first 30 days after your grandma's funeral. I have found comfort in the beard I still have, which reminds me of grandma's death and my decision not to shave during those same first 30 days.

It is clear to me now that I could not have known how I would feel when Terrie found the *kippah* my father bought for himself in Jerusalem more than 10 years ago—and that I would want to wear it from then on when I pray. I realize that we are often experimenting and sometimes adopting different Jewish rituals that help define who we are individually and as a family. Sometimes these rituals are traditional in origin, sometimes we adapt them to our own circumstances, and sometimes we have created them out of our own particular needs.

As your mom and I have often explained to you three children, our Jewish home is a much more observant one than either of us grew up in. As we grow and mature as a family we have learned what works for us. Sometimes I think that what is unique about our family is how many ways we can argue over who does what around the Shabbat dinner table, or again during Havdalah. I know that this is not unique with the Raphael family, but it is a style that we have perfected to a high art form.

With grandma's death and now grandpa's, I realize now that the lessons from my parents that remain are the ones I am able to recall upon further reflection about what they gave to me.

There are many lessons that I learned, but there are three that I want to share with you now.

The first is about my belief in God. Of course, you three children look at your father the rabbi and you are certain that belief in God is just something that comes with who and what I am. I know better, and in fact, I have tried with some difficulty to share some of my doubts and struggles with you. I have long ago learned, however, that being a parent is a much more difficult job of teaching than any classroom experience that I have ever had.

My parents never explicitly encouraged us to talk about something as difficult and as personal as what our belief in God was. I don't know if I ever told you about my father's reaction to my telling him I was planning to become a rabbi—this, of course, was when Uncle Marc was already in rabbinic school. Grandpa said, "Oh my gosh, everyone is going to think I'm religious!" In the home I grew up in there was the understanding that it was perfectly all right to ask questions about anything, including our beliefs. It was not easy, however. It wasn't until a number of years ago, after I had already become a rabbi, I came to realize that one of the things that many of us lack in this secular society is the vocabulary to discuss our own personal belief system.

My very first HUC sermon struggled with this notion of belief in a transcendent being. I remember twenty-four years ago when I used the image of Jacob's ladder to discuss my personal theology. I struggled with the notion that the contract Jacob strikes with God suggests that God is limited in acting in human history. This rational notion of a limited deity proposed that we must be responsible for our actions and deeds, but even more than that, when bad things happened there was not much point in imploring God to intervene. My emerging understanding of a power greater than us suggested that this existence of ours was part of a partnership with God. The facts of free will and choice convinced me to believe in a God who had limited involvement in our world.

Such a belief served me well for a number of years, but brought me up short almost two years ago when I hastened to California, hoping that my mother would recover from pneumonia and emerge from intensive care. I prayed to God for the recovery of my mother, but with very mixed emotions. Part of me felt that it was treating God like the "Doctor in the Sky." I was not seeking a relationship with God which would help determine my purpose as a Jew. I was not seeking closeness and was not trying to understand how I stood in a covenantal relationship between God and the Jewish people. All the things that I had believed, and I had preached about as a rabbi, starting slipping from my grasp.

I was seeking supernatural intervention, not the God of gradualness, of the slow natural cycle of earth. I wanted the God of splitting seas, of thunder, and of all-powerfulness. I wanted my mother to recover and live. Yet I did not believe that God worked that way.

For many years, when I silently prayed at services, I pictured a series of concentric circles. The smallest one was our family, next came the community we live in, next came the Jewish people, Israel, and then came all of humanity. I thought about these circles when I closed my eyes and meditated on the meaning of love and peace. I did not pray that God would intervene and cure some particular circle in that constellation; rather, I acknowledged these circles as part of the definition of who I was as an individual, as a Jew, and as a member of the human race.

I have seen too many sick people who deserved to be cured, who prayed and hoped, and who still died, to have confidence in God intervening in such matters. I believe that God has created a natural universe and though malignancies occur in this natural order, God has given us humans the power, the ability, the thought processes to strive to continuously uncover the cures for such malignancies. God will not reach down and rearrange the development of the human body to accommodate me because of the fervency of my prayer—or the deservedness of my mother.

Still I prayed. Part of my desperation (and now I realize even more, my understanding) is to take refuge in long shots. Who knows? I certainly don't have all the answers, I don't even know if I have all the questions. All these rational theological views could be wrong. Perhaps God not only listens, but acts. Perhaps the heavens not only have ears, but arms.

So while sitting in the Dallas airport between planes that morning, I prayed. While in the ICU waiting room, I prayed, and who knows why my mother lived for another 12 months? My rational belief and certainty has been checked some, and now when I pray silently I usually only think about my parents.

Many outside of the small world of rabbinic school think that rabbis and rabbinic students have fully worked through their belief systems, arrived at a definitive answer, and are ready and able to articulate such beliefs to others. Long ago I realized that this is not the case, but in fact, most students and many rabbis are anxious and deeply suspicious of talking about their belief. We easily convince ourselves that everyone else knows with certainty about God, has developed a sound and systematic theology, and therefore any admission that our own belief is in the process of "becoming" is withheld in the hopes that no one else will discover such shortcomings. This often successfully inhibits possible discussion of our own theological struggles.

Rachel, when I was 7, I was also trying to understand what all these stories and what all these experiences with Judaism meant to me. Andrew, when I was 9, I was also asking questions about the ultimate meaning of the universe, where do good and evil come from, and what is the truth about whether Queen Esther and Mordecai, Moses and Pharaoh really existed? Matthew, when I was 14, I was also resentful of my parents forcing me to go to religious school, and worse, to services!! That certainly was not how I wanted to spend my time.

Thinking about what I was like at those ages has enabled me to think about the second matter I want to discuss with you in this ethical will. The second legacy that I hope to leave to all three of you is the burning desire to learn more. Like most Jewish parents, my mother and father treasured learning and particularly encouraged their three children to take the fullest advantage of whatever learning we could.

I remember the day when my older brother graduated from college and my father proudly announced that his son was the very first in the family to ever accomplish this task. These outward measurements were only part of the story in our home. My mother would have become a social worker if she'd had the opportunity for higher education. My father thought he would have liked to have been a school teacher. Their life stories made these two goals unobtainable, but they worked hard to help us realize ours.

The legacy from them that I hope to share with you three children is a legacy long-treasured by the Jewish people. Our ancestors knew that learning was something that no one could ever take away from you. The quest for knowledge, the love of learning, the seeking after the unknown and mastering it, these are important attributes that I hope you will always hold dear. Your parents both decided that learning and formal education are an extremely high value and one that we made significant sacrifices to accomplish.

Matthew, you remember the doctoral studies of both your mother and father; Andrew and Rachel, you have only lived through mine. All of you have become used to seeing one or both of your parents reading, writing, and, as my mother used to say, when I was much younger, "making our lessons."

I first wrote this ethical will at a time of great hope for

many in this country. We eagerly looked ahead to the possible accomplishments of the new Clinton administration. Much has happened in our country as well as Israel and the Middle East since then. Now things are not quite the same, but my original words, which I wrote at the end of 1992, still express my deepest yearnings. Children, as you grow up in this world, I hope education will help you not to be led astray by people who want you to believe that there is only one side to every story. Whether it be strife great enough to cause bloodshed and the loss of life, or strife small enough to cause heartbreak and unhappiness, strife often occurs when two sides cannot agree. An educated and inquisitive mind, as well as healthy skepticism, that leads you beyond easy and convenient answers, this is the necessary antidote for these attempts at delusion.

There is a third legacy from my parents that I want to share with you. Perhaps because there were many relatives around when I was growing up, perhaps because I am a middle child, perhaps for many other reasons that I am unaware, I feel compelled to warn you about the pitfalls of false pride. I think I learned some years ago how important it is to be able to benefit from all. In the Talmud (Ta'anit 7a) Rav Hanina is quoted as saying: "I have learnt much from my teachers, and from my colleagues more than from my teachers, but from my students more than from them all."

Who are my students? Some of the them are at Hebrew Union College. Everyday I encounter students who teach me something new. Some days I learn more from them about what it feels like to be overwhelmed; some days I learn more about what the important questions are that must be asked; some days I learn what a special caring relationship exists amongst the people who are studying to be educators, cantors, and rabbis; some days I learn more about how to take our tradition of *tzedekah* and *gemilut ḥasadim* seriously enough to live our lives infused with concerns of people less fortunate than ourselves.

You, my three children, have taught me more than anyone. Through all the pitfalls, dangers, traumas, and difficulties of parenthood, I have discovered how much there is to learn. I have learned that being a husband and a father is life's most challenging and most rewarding task. I have learned about the uniqueness of humans beings—the differences in us even though we are all created in God's image—and even though three of you come from the same set of parents.

Rachel, you continue to teach me that youngest is not ever less but sometimes more; that girl is not always soft but often quite resilient, that small is rarely ever weak and frequently very tough. It was you, you may recall, who was most able to put into words what everyone was feeling after learning of my mother's death. I remember you saying that if grandma died, then so could mom. It was a frightening thought for all of us, but that realization—as scary as it was, and is, to contemplate—encouraged all of us to talk, and to listen to the thoughts and feelings of each other.

Andrew, I have learned much from you. You as the middle child, with an older brother and younger sister; you who find a way of getting along with everyone; you who are largely satisfied with whatever life deals you; you who are the one that seems to ask the questions that really make the rest of us reach. How you can strike right at the heart of the matter is an uncanny ability you have. I remember you saying to me, "Dad, when I am as old as you are, I hope you will still be alive." So do I Andrew, so do I.

Matthew, you are our firstborn who has grown so much. You continue to make us proud of your mastery of life. Nothing comes easy for you, but you engage us each and every hour of every day. Do you remember that at grandma's funeral you said, "She always expressed her feelings"? Well, there is some of that in you, as well. The direct, honest, and forthright person that you are reminds me how wonderful being your father is to me.

I want to return to relationships and repeat to you a story I have read in several different places. The story will hopefully illustrate a point I have been trying to make about who we are and why we exist in relationship and dependent upon one another.

Once upon a time, a woman was in purgatory until she had fulfilled the expiation of her sins. After the woman was finally cleansed, the messenger came to lift her from the lowest depths to the height of heaven. The messenger put the end of a slim branch in the woman's hand and said, "Hold fast to this branch, and I will pull you up."

The woman seized the end of the branch and clung to it fiercely, as the messenger rose and began to lift her upwards. The woman passed others who were in these same depths: hands were outstretched toward her, and voices said pleadingly, "Take us with you." The woman answered, "Grab on. The branch will hold us all."

So they clutched at her, one seizing her by the arm, another by the skirt, and another about the waist. But miraculously, no one fell, and the odd-looking group moved steadily higher, closer to their goal, supported by the branch which was as a link between the woman and the messenger.

Then suddenly the woman became afraid and she said to herself, "There are too many! The branch will break. It cannot support all of us."

And she began to kick and turn, to shake off those holding her. She shouted, "Let go! Get off! It's my branch. It's my branch."

As the words "my branch" crossed her lips, the branch broke and the woman tumbled back to where she had begun.

The branch was strong enough for all when she said, "It will hold us." It was too weak, even for her, when she said, "my branch."

I want to share these final thoughts in my ethical will:

We are all in this grand mystery of life together. Life is too short and this planet is too small for any one of us to hold the branch and ignore all the others who dwell here. All of us have been created in God's image, and we need to be sensitive to God's great world, to be filled with wonder about our infinite capacity to learn and to grow, and we need to understand that our joy and our ability to be transformed can come from anyone, anytime, anywhere.

I pray that I may continue to see each of you grow in your happiness, your caring for one another, and your Jewishness. I hope that as you grow older you might hold onto these words which I spoke about grandma at her funeral,

"My mother was one of the least pretentious persons I have ever known. She truly disliked pretense. She also sought simplicity in her life. She knew that what was important was how people behaved and not who they knew or what they had acquired in life. She sought to acquire very little and was attached to very few material objects. Her physical needs were simple. She ate simple foods; she dressed in a straightforward fashion. She wanted who she was, not what she could buy, to be her statement."

May this memory of your grandma be part of your inheritance. I pray with all my heart and from the deepest of my soul, may God grant me and your mom, Terrie, the good fortune and good health to see you continue to grow and to revise this will many times over in the years to come.

With much love,
Your Father

In the almost two years that have passed since I wrote this will, I have often found myself reflecting upon the words and the beliefs that I expressed. Most often I think about this during prayer. My spiritual journey continues down the same path that I have indicated, the roadblocks are many, and the setbacks are frequent. I am still searching for new vocabulary words to increase my spiritual vocabulary. I still find myself struggling with the dichotomy between the rational and the nonrational self inside my being. The concentric circles still haunt my visions when I close my eyes and still my voice. My prayers are no longer primarily directed to keeping my mother or my father alive, rather they are focused on other ones whom I am in relationship with and then the larger concentric circles of community and the Jewish people.

My thinking is that I will not be asking for divine intervention, not asking for God's arms to pick up and embrace, until the next time that the life of one of my loved ones is threatened.

Talmud Torah and Spirituality: A Postmodern Perspective

Joshua Saltzman
Dedicated to the memory of Emmanuel Levinas, z'l

I. A Journey into Postmodernity

Many American Jews are preoccupied with the subject. It is part of the contemporary Jewish *zeitgeist*. Spirituality! What does it mean to talk about it in a specifically Jewish context?[1] How do we find it? Who really has it? Are there any false prophets and idolatrous, syncretistic practices informing its wholesale distribution? And perhaps most importanty, what does it tell us about the direction and reconstitution of Judaism as we approach the twenty-first century?

Countless Jews of all ages are looking to answer these questions in almost every imaginable guise. The spectrum of alternatives and offerings almost boggles the mind.

137

Anything and everything—from new age healing to popular mystical disciplines—is considered legitimately within the bounds of "Jewish spirituality" once these two trendy words are (im)properly affixed to a person, place, book, practice or idea.

Curiously, one direction that has received relatively little attention is the place of Talmud Torah (the study of Torah)[2] in the ongoing discussion of Jewish spirituality. Yet historically, Talmud Torah and Jewish spirituality were inextricably linked and understood as the single most important vehicle for the transmission of Jewish values, beliefs and practices.[3] I believe that Talmud Torah must play a central role in any

---

1. The question of whether "spirituality" as it is commonly understood in contemporary Jewish circles reflects an authentic mode of Jewish spiritual expression is an important issue to address. In "Judaism and the Search for Spiritiuality," *Conservative Judaim*, Vol. 38(2), 1985–6: 5, Neil Gillman suggests that the term spiritiuality "reflects a dualistic view of the human being which is more Platonic and Christian than biblical and rabbinic. It implies a debasement of the human body . . . it denies the meaningfulness of human activity in the social and interpersonal realms of this world. . . . In other words, is not the current search for spirituality one more example of the nefarious attempt to bring to bear Western (read: Greek and Christian) categories of thought on authentically Jewish (read: biblical and rabbinic) forms of religious expression." Nevertheless, the fact remains that spiritiuality is on the agenda. As Gillman suggests, perhaps we need to redefine the frame of reference, to introduce and speak to the Western world of the uniquely particular mélange of voices which emerge from Jewish spirituality.

2. Construed in the broadest sense of both written and oral Torah.

3. In "From the Congregational School to the Learning Congregation: Are We Ready for a Paradigm Shift?" in Isa Aron, Sara Lee and Seymour Rossel, eds., *A Congregation of Learners: Transforming the Synagogue Into a Learning Community* (New York: UAHC Press, 1995), pp. 56–78, Isa Aron writes: "According to the tradition, Jewish learning is necessary not because it helps one perform better on the job or because it leads to self-improvement but because it engages one's spiritual and moral sensibilities. And the traditional mode of Jewish learning is, by definition, communal. In the process of learning, the Jewish community is re-created and reinvigorated."

ongoing and serious dialogue concerning the question of Jewish spirituality today.

That Talmud Torah quintessentially embodies Jewish spirituality is one of the key points in Robert Gibbs' explanation of Emmanuel Levinas' profound committment to Jewish education. Torah study is the single most significant response for Levinas to a whole host of profoundly disturbing issues raised by modernity and assimilation, Gibbs states, reflecting further that "Levinas demands that Jewish education offer a teaching from its resources that will make Judaism not merely an ethnicity worthy of preservation, nor even a nationality in need of survival, but ultimately 'the unique means to preserve humanity and the personality of man.'"[4] Levinas, continues Gibbs, challenges the unimaginable suffering and destruction of modernity by calling for a radical reorientation of our responsibility to others.

> For Levinas the crisis of Nazism requires that Jewish thought be made available for the general culture, and that Judaism can offer what is most lacking: The insight into a moral responsiblity which extends beyond the bounds of my own action. What Europe and the West most need to learn is that I am responsible even for the actions that are perpetrated against me, even for the violence of my persecutors. Levinas discovers this teaching of radical responsibility, of unchosen obligations, of a fundemental social solidarity, within the traditions of Jewish classical texts.[5]

4. Robert Gibbs, "Blowing on the Embers: Two Jewish Works of Emmanuel Levinas," in *Modern Judaism* 14 (1994): 106.
5. Ibid., p. 101.

In asserting the key role of Jewish texts in the reorientation of Jewish life for Levinas, Gibbs is also making a profound statement about the importance of Talmud Torah in
postmodernity. He writes: "To engage in Jewish education,
for the sake of Jewish survival and as a contribution to our
postmodern world, is to discover what Judaism has been."[6]
He goes on to note that for Levinas, "the task of teaching
becomes relevant but not redundant for the West capable of
Hitler, Stalin, atom bombs, genocide, and ecological
destruction. . . . The key resourses are texts. . . . He prefers
the old texts, in part because they admit of many readings,
in part because they hold wonders of which most of us are
ignorant, and most of all becasue they address and explore
the responsibilities we have. Discourse, discussion, written
argument—these describe a mode of holiness which resides
in these texts and just because the ethical relations between
human beings are constituted through these linguistic practices and human beings are constituted through these linguistic practices . . . Levinas demands that we all learn more
about how to read the texts."[7]

Levinas finds the key to spirituality in the recovery of
Jewish texts and in their study. But how exactly is this particular notion of postmodernity to be understood and what
is it about Talmud Torah that makes it such a uniquely Jewish spiritual enterprise?

Stephen Kepnes has written an important article on post-

---

6. Ibid., p. 106.
7. Ibid., p. 104.

modern Judaism which appears in a recently published text he edited[8] entitled "Postmodern Interpretations of Judaism: Deconstructive and Constructive Approaches."[9] Kepnes also asserts that the postmodern age is a response to the failures and limits of modernity. Modernity, particularly its component of Jewish assimilation which brought it into contact with the most heineous and awesome evil the world has ever seen as well as its remarkable contributions and benefits, failed to provide an adequate religious and cultural lifestyle to the challenges raised by Jewish emancipation and enlightenment.

Postmodern Judaism, like postmodernity and its array of radical critical theories, is not a complete repudiation of modernity but rather a recognition of modernity's profound ethical and spiritual fracturing. Postmodernity seeks to reconstitute the political, cultural and religious realms. It does so by carefully listening to the "voices of the other" that were rendered silent by a ruthless modernity. Countless peoples, differentiated by race, religion, gender, sexual preference or age were marginalized, ostracized and in many cases eradictated from the face of the earth in the unceasing and relentless march toward scientific and technological progress. The world and its people were there to be conquered. Postmodern Judaism(s) is one among a number of voices reaching out of the long and dark night of modernity's violent conquest.

---

8. *Interpreting Judaism in a Postmodern Age,* ed. Stephen Kepnes (New York and London: New York University Press, 1996).

9. Ibid., p. 1–18.

Kepnes writes that postmodernity calls for a transformation of the epistemological assumptions of the modern world. He rejects the notion of "objective" knowledge which established a nefarious link between "science and the humanities . . . the dream of modernity has been to use technical and calculating reason to subsume all reality under objective universal law and thereby achieve increasing domination and control of the natural and human worlds."[10] Postmodernity abandons the dream of "objective" knowledge. Instead, it focuses on the particularities of the human subject, existing in a particular place, at a particular time and within a particular historical context. These particularites produce the possibility of knowledge. They, as it were, construct our reality.

This notion of the postmodern is helpful in understanding a particular stream of contemporary Jewish exploration which I like to refer to as postmodern Jewish ethics and which has a direct relation to Talmud Torah. In this context, the study of Torah is not simply the acquisition of knowledge but becomes something more akin to the art of knowing. Susan Handelman asks the following question: if knowledge is always informed by ideological predispositions of our constructed world, then "dosen't every theory or account of knowing also have an implied pedagogy? . . . Or, put still another way, is teaching not only the conveying of knowledge, but itself a way of knowing in excess of what it conveys?"[11] If this is the case, our understanding of Tal-

---

10. Ibid., p. 9.

mud Torah can now be approached from a very different perspective. The relationship between the teacher, student and text in the world of Torah study[12] would then be seen to differ radically from Western notions of knowledge, pedagogy and study. The uniquely Jewish spiritual model of pedagogy to which Handelman refers has much to contribute to the world at large.

II. Rubrics of Talmud Torah as a Spiritual Encounter

1. Study, Spirituality and Ethics

R. Tarfon and the Sages were assembled in the upper chamber of the house of Nitzah in Lydda. This question was asked of them: Is study greater or is practice greater? R. Tarfon answered, 'Practice is greater.' R. Akiva answered, 'Study is greater.' They [the others] all called out and said, 'Study is greater, for study leads to practice.'[13]

At least at a first glance the quote cited above suggests that for the rabbinic sages study is not only the supreme value of Jewish living but is also the ultimate form of Jewish religiousity. It is not simply an excercise in intellectual refinement; study is the definition of Jewish spirituality.

Jewish spirituality is a complex structure. At its most fundemental level, as shown in the passage above, the question is raised about the relative importance of study versus

---

11. Ibid., p. 222.
12. Throughout this essay, Torah refers to the entire corpus of sacred Jewish texts and study includes both traditional modes of Jewish learning and interpretation as well as contemporary critical hermeneutical practices.
13. BT Kiddushin 40b.

practice. Norman Lamm, in his book, *Torah Lishma: Torah for Torah's Sake in the Works of Rabbi Hayyim of Volozhin and his Contemporaries*[14] traces the history of the scholarly and rabbinic opinions concerning the debate on this issue between R. Akiva and R. Tarfon. He suggests one way of understanding the rabbinic view is that the "preference for study is meant only in a chronological sense; it is to be pro-paedeutic to practice."[15]

However, his discussion of Rabbi Hayyim of Volozhin (R. Hayyim) sheds light on the fact that study includes practice. Lamm emphasizes that it was R. Hayyim almost alone, among the followers of the Lurianic mystical tradition, who understood the Torah as preexisting creation in the supernal, unknowable, region of Ein-Sof. Torah in this view, adds Lamm, "is conceived of as an aspect of God Himself, in His absoluteness and transcendence."[16] Thus, he explains, this is one of the several reasons why R. Hayyim valued the study of Torah above all else. R. Hayyim understood the debate in Lydda as emphasizing a) the fact that only through study can one come to understand all of the mitzvot b) halakhically, Torah study is also a mitzvah or form of practice to lead one to God. Mitzvah is indeed the experience of God through the doing of the commandments.

But for R. Hayyim, these are primarily normative, hala-

14. Norman Lamm, *Torah Lishmah: Torah for Torah's Sake in the Works of Rabbi Hayyim of Volozhin and his Contemporaries* (Hoboken, New Jersey: Ktav Publishing House, Inc., 1989).
15. Ibid., p. 141.
16. Ibid., p. 105.

khic concerns. The real issue is formulated in different terms. From a mystical point of view "Torah is the whole of which the mitzvot are only the individual parts. . . . 'The study of Torah equals all the other [commandments combined]' . . . is not merely an equation of value but an inclusion of all the other commandments within the mystical organism of Torah."[17]

What may appear to be mere mystical speculation is in fact a radical reorientation of the mystical toward the ethical.[18] R. Hayyim learns from the Zohar that God created human beings as a mystical microcosm of the supra-mundane/Divine realm. Within the mystical body all the secrets of the worlds (mystical worlds) are contained. He arrives at this startling conclusion through a commentary on the meaning of "And Elokim created man in His own image" found in Genesis 1:27. In a marvelous essay partially dealing with this commentary[19] Richard Cohen explains that by focusing on the name of "Elokim" used for God in the Genesis passage, R. Hayyim "reminds us, in contrast to the many other possible names used in used in the Bible to designate God"[20] that "Elokim" alludes to the "master of all powers." It is as Elokim that God creates and gives human beings

---

17. Ibid., p. 155.

18. See Richard A. Cohen, *Elevations: The Height of the Good in Rosenzweig and Levinas* (Chicago and London: The University of Chicago Press, 1994), pp. 267–273 for a fuller elaboration of the relationship between R. Hayyim's mysticism and ethics.

19. Ibid., p. 268.

20. Ibid., p. 268.

dominon "over myriads of powers and over numberless-worlds."[21]

The central thrust of R. Hayyim's commentary is that creation in the image of Elokim bestows upon human beings a mastery which is similiar to God's; namely, that "the perfection of the divine realm now depends on the perfection of human behavior."[22] Hence the study of Torah is not only a vehicle for mystical speculation but according to R. Hayyim, it assumes a form of radical ethics. Human ethical behavior becomes tantamount to determining the "orderliness of the cosmic order, its goodness."[23] Torah study is the ultimate form of praxis, for through it one uncovers a mystical ethical imperative which potentially redeems the universe. The value of Torah study is transformed from a purely intellectual, insular pursuit into a spirituality of ethics on the highest order of our humanity. R. Hayyim writes: "there is no comparison or similiarity at all between the holiness and the light of the commandments and *the power of the holiness and light of the holy Torah,* which radiates its light upon the man who engages and *meditates on it in the proper fashion* [my emphasis]."[24] And elsewhere he adds "The real truth is . . . that the World to Come is actually identical with man's own deeds; it is that portion which he expanded, added and prepared by his own efforts."[25]

21. R. Hayyim of Volozhin, *Nefesh Hahayim,* ch. 1:3
22. Ibid., p. 268.
23. Ibid., p. 269.
24. R. Hayyim of Volozhin, *Nefesh Hahayim,* ch. 4:30.
25. Ibid., ch.1:12.

2. Hermeneutics and Pedagogy

Another aspect of the spirituality of Talmud Torah revolves around the act of interpretation itself. Handelman connects the act of midrashic hermeneutics to midrashic pedagogy. She suggests that the "pedagogical self-consciouness of midrash" is in part a function of its oral, homiletic origins. The teleos of the interpetive midrashic act for the rabbis was directed towards "normative instruction". The key to this notion is "the relation of rabbinic hermeneutics to rabbinic pedagogy."[26] The nexus between the rabbinic interpretive act as a revelatory moment and the rabbi's role as teacher, explains Handelman, is illustrated in the textual dialogue which occurs within the midrashic/talmudic framework. The text is the site of a continual "dialogue and debate of teachers" and hence allows us to enact the transmission of knowledge through "the teaching relation." The infinite production of interpretations by the rabbis, understood as the "word of God . . . is to continue Sinai, to reenact the revelation, by uncovering those meanings."[27] Thus, Torah study must be understood first and foremost as the ongoing revelation of God.

Moreover, as Marc-Alain Ouaknin believes:

the ideas of the interpreter are, from the very start, involved in revitalizing the meaning of the text; his personal background is a decisive factor. But it is not so in terms of a

---

26. Susan Handelman, "The 'Torah' of Criticism" in *Interpreting Judaism in a Postmodern Age,* p. 229.

27. Ibid., p. 230.

personal point of view that would be maintained or imposed but, rather, like an opinion or a possibility that comes into play, allowing one to apply the content of the text to oneself.[28]

The interpretive act not only makes the text relevant to the existential situation of its readers but in the process of interpretation the student/teacher praticipates in the "divine-human dialogue." Study and interpretation of the text become pedagogic practices by which students learn to become teachers and are empowered to carry on the tradition to the "broader Jewish society."[29] Therefore, Torah study is also critical for our survival as a people. It functions as the vehicle for the transmission of Jewish knowledge, values and practice from one generation to another. The study of Torah is a pedagogy which "teaches us how it must be taught . . . The content of its teaching is inseperable from the form of its teaching."[30]

Another important dimension of study as pedagogy is the relationship and dialogue which is established between students in the *hevruta* (study partnership) system. The Mishnah states that "if two sit together and no words of Torah are exchanged between them this is a company of scoffers. . . . But two who sit together and the words of Torah are exchanged between them, the Divine Presence abides with them."[31] That is to say, the dialogic nature of *hevruta*

---

28. Mark-Alain Ouaknin, *The Burnt Book: Reading the Talmud* trans. Llewellyn Brown (Princeton, New Jersey: Princeton University Press, 1995), p. 59.

29. Handelman, "The 'Torah' of Criticism," p. 230.

30. Ibid., p. 230.

study can potentially transform the relationship between students into an encounter with the Divine. But this only occurs when the act of study is focused not only on Torah but on the responsibility, concern and spiritual presence of the other study partner.

Studying together is a teaching of our ethical obligation to the "other" and through it a revelation of the Divine "Other". The *hevruta* is a spiritual act of openess—of learning how to listen and respond with compassion and interest—one is both student and teacher. If this does not occur, claims the Mishnah, the students become "scoffers". Instead of imbuing the relationship with the Divine, the students are concerned solely with their own needs and concerns—a self-referential monologue. The student remains imprisoned in the clutches of the ego. For R. Hayyim (see above), as for Levinas, the inability to fully engage in the dialogue of study is not simply a failure of communication but the loss of the redemptive possibility of Talmud Torah. The stakes are infinitely high. The *hevruta* may either enact a repair (*tikkun*) or destruction (*shevirah*) of the cosmic order. This, I believe, is the ultimate ethical/spiritual import of what studying together as partners in *hevruta* may accomplish.

3. The Teacher-Student Relationship: Models of Jewish Spirituality

When I first came to the Hebrew Union College-Jewish Institute of Religion (HUC-JIR) in New York as a rabbinic

---

31. *Pirke Avot* 3:3.

student, I was repeatedly warned by a variety of individuals that if I were looking for spirituality—look elswhere! And it is true, HUC-JIR is an institution like any other with many concerns and in the past, the least of which was the spiritual search of its students. Yes, you receive your required Judaic background, training in professional development, opportunities to lead services and give sermons. But God forbid you should look for some down-to-earth spiritual enrichment.

"Hey, we are training rabbis here, not gurus" I heard the collective institutional voice saying to me. HUC-JIR must also decide whether it is a graduate or rabbinic school. But to its credit, the College-Institute is working toward a remedy of this problematic dichotomy. In fact, nowadays, you often hear HUC-JIR being refered to as a "yeshiva." That is a radical change in perspective! Yet, as Michael Goldberg wrote in an essay referring to the Jewish Theological Seminary but which also applies here, one still wonders whether it is an insult to accidently address a faculty member as "Rabbi instead of Doctor."[32]

At any rate, it did not come as a great suprise to me when I found myself starving for some sort of spiritual, personal dimension. I was lucky. There are a few rabbis around on the faculty and even some who are willing to talk about belief in God and spirituality.

In my first class in Jewish theology I found my Rabbi at

---

32. Michael Goldberg, "Discipleship: Basing One Life on Another—It's Not What You Know, It's Who You Know," in *Theology Without Foundations: Religious Practice and the Future of Theological Truth,* eds. Stanley Hauerwas, Nancy Murphy and Mark Nation (Nashville: Abingdon Press, 1994), p. 299.

HUC-JIR. I have to admit that I was expecting to find one of the leading Jewish liberal theologians of our time, Rabbi Eugene Borowitz, a little distant, the academic sort, perhaps even frightening. But the first thing he said to me as we went around the class introducing ourselves was "I know your Dad. We were in jail together with Dr. King in the South." That is not typically what you expect to hear from a professor of Theology. It was the beginning of a long and enduring relationship that has profoundly influenced my intellectual, emotional and spiritual development.

Rabbi Borowitz began his remarks in class by explaining that he too was concerned about the question of how to make our study of theology into something more than an academic exercise. After all, we were being trained to be rabbis. Placing a *kippah* on his head, he began to recite the blessing said before the study of Torah.[33] I knew intuitively that the spirituality I had been so desperately seeking might be found partially in this classroom with this rabbi. Don't get me wrong; Rabbi Borowitz demanded rigorous, analytic thinking from all of us. He does abide sloppy thinking. But his teaching style is unique. He actually engages the student in a dialogue of mutual question and debate.

"Classically," writes Goldberg, "students of the Jewish tradition were called talmidei chachamim—'students of the wise' . . . Hence, what title or term of address could have better suited that personal relationship of a student to a sage than 'Rabbi'—'My Master'?"[34] Rabbi Borowitz became my "master" not so much by the knowledge he imparted, though I learned a great deal from him, but by his actions.

He taught me Torah as much by "embodying it" as he did in "discoursing about it."[35] He embodies a spiritual model of *hochma*—Jewish wisdom.

---

33. Traditionally, one says the blessing for the study of Torah only once a day, in the morning service since the command to study Torah is in effect all day long. It is assumed that one will study Torah at some other time in the day and therefore obivates the need to repeat the blessing again. However, I believe that a number of arguments can be made which call this traditional "assumption" into question. 1) Most of us don't have a chance to say the prayer in the morning on a daily basis. If we do, we may not have another chance to study Torah during the day. Repeating the blessing whenever we do study Torah reminds us of the divine dimension of our study. 2) We are commanded in the blessing to study the *Torah l'shma* (for the sake of Torah). While many of us teach or study professionally, this is clearly not the same thing as studying Torah *l'shma*. Isa Aron writes: "The classical Jewish notion of *Torah Lishma* is based on an entirely different conception of motivation—that study is its own reward. For halachic Jews who have a more explicit worldview . . . the study of Torah (both written and oral) is a *mitzvah*. For liberal Jews the rewards must be found in the domain of the implicit, the realm of personal meaning. If we accept the concept of Torah Lishma, our goal is for learners to value the study of Torah (construed more broadly) as a vital activity because it serves to enrich their spiritual and communal lives." Isa Aron, "From the Congregational School to the Learning Congregation" in *A Congregation of Learners* eds. Isa Aron, Sara Lee, and Seymour Rossel (New York: UAHC Press, 1995), p. 72–3.) 3) We ask God to "sweeten the words of Your Torah in our mouth and the mouth of your people." One could say that metaphorically we not only eat the Torah but that from a rabbinic perspective, prayer substitutes words for food, i.e., the Temple sacrifices. Therefore, just as we say a prayer every time we literally eat food, so too, we should say a prayer every time we metaphorically eat Torah and receive sustenance from its wisdom. We literally ingest the words of Torah, just as Ezekiel, who was commanded by God to "eat this scroll, and go and speak to the house of Israel."(Ezekiel 3:1) 4) Which brings me to my final point. We conclude the blessing with the hope that "our offspring, and the offspring of your people" should know the "Name" of God and "study Your Torah." Ultimately, this is an act of renewal and redemption. By bringing the words of Torah to the next generation we renew the living covenant with God which promises the continuity of generations. The next generation also renews our lives by bringing new insights to our old ways of doing things, our habitual ways of thinking. They challenge the tyranny of fossilized behavior, rituals and institutions. Finally, by bestowing the words of Torah on future generations, we participate in the continual process of redeeming the world. We enact and practice the spiritual model of *Tikkun Olam*.

Handelman's discussion of Jewish pedagogy suggests that the teaching model can be an act of creative withdrawal drawing on the mystical, Lurianic notion of *tzimtzum* (contraction). She explains that Luria introduced a radical new way of understanding God and the act of creation. "God had to 'contract' himself, so to speak, in order to allow a 'space' for finite creation to occur. A teacher, the analogy goes, must perform the same kind of act."[36] Rather ironically, approximately twenty years earlier, Rabbi Borowitz wrote a very similiar essay called "*Tzimtzum*: A Mystical Model for Contemporary Leadership"[37] which Handelman neither quotes nor cites.

Both Handelman and Rabbi Borowitz understand that for a teacher to convey knowledge, a "contraction" must take place to create a space for the student to learn to digest the knowledge being conveyed. Handelman also suggests that just as *tzimtzum* precedes and allows the act of creation to take place, so too, the space created by the teacher's contraction makes a space for the dialogue of the student and teacher to begin. The transmission of knowledge is made possible in an act of creative contraction.

This process of opening and contraction has another important dimension which is treated by Mark-Alain

34. Ibid., p. 291.
35. See Goldberg's essay for a further elaboration of this fundemental difference.
36. Handelman, "The 'Torah' of Criticism," p. 233.
37. Eugene Borowitz, "Tzimtzum: A Mystic Model for Contemprary Leadership" in *Exploring Jewish Ethics: Papers on Covenant Responsibility* (Detroit: Wayne State University, 1990), pp. 320–331.

Ouaknin.[38] Ouaknin comments on a talmudic passage[39] in which an argument is being waged over the question of whether a verse from of the book of Joshua which reads: "And Joshua wrote these words in the book of the law of Elohim" (Joshua 24:26) actually indicate that he added to the words of Moses in the Torah itself. One side of the argument opines that this verse alludes to a passage in the Torah which Joshua included but which was already written by Moses. The alternative argument bodly asserts that Joshua added eight new verses to the Torah. However, the crux of the the argument, writes Ouaknin, is the problem of "opening" and the "transmission of opening"—which is perhaps one of the fundamental teachings of Judaism. Joshua represents the figure of the disciple, as such, the Master (Moses) had to make way for him, had to withdraw from before him . . . The Master understands—even if it is hard for him—that he must leave and this absence begins with the impossibility of writing with visible ink. It is the disciple who finishes the book of the Master. But who is the Master? And who is the Disciple?[40]

Ouaknin understands the withdrawal of the Master as a mode of transmission. The disciple interrupts the totality (authority of the tradition, teacher and text) by an opening which refuses to close the text. Interpretation and transmission co-mingle in the infinite re-reading and re-writing of the sacred texts of our tradition.

38. Mark-Alain Ouaknin, *The Burnt Book: Reading the Talmud,* trans. Llewellyn Brown (Princeton, New Jersey: Princeton Univeristy Press, 1995), pp. 12–13.
39. BT *Bava Batra* 15a
40. Marc-Alain Ouaknin, *The Burnt Book,* p. 13.

I will conclude this essay by relating a personal incident which occurred severeal years ago. After I was ordained, I was hospitilized for a short period of time. As soon as he was informed of my hospitalization, Rabbi Borowitz travelled many hours to visit me. His was an act of of *bikkur holim* (visiting the sick). He sat with me for hours and he just listened. He simply listened to my words. He came to be with me. He listened to my pain, my rage, my confession. From this I learned the spiritual models of *hakshava* (attentive listening); *rachmanut* (compassion) and most of all the possibility of the master (teacher)-disciple (student) relationship as potentially messinaic.[41] Emmanuel Levinas writes: "The experience in which the messianic personality is revealed . . . comes back to the relationship between student and teacher. The student-teacher relationship, which seemingly remains rigorously intellectual, contains all the riches of a meeting with the Messiah."[42]

In the meeting with the other/teacher the messianic moment appears. The Talmud relates the story of R. Yehoshua ben Levi's encounter with Elijah. R. Yehoshua asks Elijah when the Messiah will finally come. Elijah responds by enjoining him to go ask the Messiah himself. Elijah directs him to the gates of Rome where "he is sitting among the poor who are stricken with illnesses."[43] R. Yehoshua rushes to the gates of Rome and there he finds the Messiah tending his own personal wounds.

---

41. See Handelman's essay on the teacher-student relation as messianic.
42. Emmanuel Levinas, *Difficult Freedom: Essays on Judaism,* trans. Sean Hand (Baltimore: Johns Hopkins University Press, 1990), p. 85.
43. BT Sanhedrin 98a

He greets the Messiah and asks him, "When will you come O master?" "Today" was the Messiah's answer.

But R. Yehoshua is confounded by this answer and returns to Elijah to ask whether the Messiah has in fact spoken falsely. The Messiah said he would come today and he has not, charges R. Yehoshua. Elijah responds, "When he told you, 'Today', he was quoting the first word of a verse (Psalms 95:6) that goes on to say, 'If you will hear his voice.'"[44]

Levinas suggests that with all the suffering of the Messiah who is ready to come and even with the suffering of humanity, it is not enough to bring the Messiah and save humanity. All depends upon humanity's response to suffering. The teacher/student relationship may bring the Messiah if only they accept the infinite responsiblity they share for one another. This is the ultimate spiritual ideal of Talmud Torah.

---

44. Ibid.

Hineni—Ehyeh Asher Ehyeh

Nancy Wiener

Notwithstanding all the theological problems of anthropomorphism presented by the concept, it is the whole man [*sic*], body and mind, instinct and spirit, that was created in God's image and as such in his [*sic*] complex entirety, represents that image on this earth.[1]

S *hema Yisrael Adonai Eloheinu, Adonai Ehad.* God is one—complex, yet unified and whole. Jews affirm this daily. I affirm this daily. I believe that humans are created in God's image and likeness, and I believe that we are each born with a unique essence that is the godliness in us. Like God we are ultimately complex and unified. We understand that these attributes can coexist in God. However, we, created in God's image, often have trouble recognizing these attributes in ourselves and accepting them as an essential

---

1. Eliezer Berkovitz, *Crisis and Faith* (New York: Sanhedrin Press, 1976), p. 51.

part of our being. We have the potential to manifest our own godliness when we bring our entire being integrated complexity into the world.

In Genesis we read that God summons Adam with the question *Ayekah?*—"Where are you?" Adam does not say, "Here, next to the tree." Nor does he say, "I don't know." Rather, he answers where he is in relation to God. We, too, are asked *Ayekah?* Our answer, all too often, is limited to our location in space. We, all too often, fail to answer such a question with a response that reflects our understanding of our relationship to the world, to God, to others, and to our selves.

What would it take to be able to answer *Ayekah?* with *Hineni*—"Here I am, all of me," and to say it with certainty and wholeheartedly—with *kavvanah?*

I believe that such a response is possible. This belief results from my understanding of God.

I am deeply moved by the name ascribed to God in Exodus 3:14, *Ehyeh Asher Ehyeh*. Translating the untranslatable: "I am what I am; I am what I will become; I will be what I will be." I hear this as an affirmation of God's eternality, ongoing presence, continuous unity and complexity. It succinctly captures the notion that the ways in which God is manifest in the world or becomes manifest to us can be variable—without God's integrity ever being in question. God's name describes part of God's essence.

In God's likeness, we, too, can accurately describe ourselves with the same words: *Ehyeh Asher Ehyeh*. We are ever in a state of becoming, but always capable of acting with integrity. We are complex, yet unified. Our great challenge is to allow ourselves and encourage others to be who we are and to become who we are meant to become.

> And God saw what he [*sic*] had made, and behold, it was good. However, after the creation of man [*sic*], this statement is missing. Albo explained: There are two kinds of perfection, of nature and of man [*sic*]. Nature's consists in its being, man's [*sic*] in his [*sic*] becoming.[2]

To view ourselves as whole beings with integrity even while we are constantly in the process of becoming—this is dependent on being able to appreciate our own complexity while recognizing the essential oneness, the integrity, the godliness we each possess every step along the way.

To express our godliness we must be able to embrace our many distinctive unique aspects. However, we often ignore or deny parts of ourselves. By not integrating our many facets, we do not give ourselves an opportunity to interact with the world with integrity. We never fully allow others to know us. We never fully experience the richness and joys of daily living. Soloveitchik teaches that only with our whole selves can we experience the joy of daily living.

As I learned while working as a student rabbi with a congregation for the deaf, our whole beings must be expressed when we communicate. If my message is to be understood, so my congregants taught me, my hands, my face, and my whole body should convey a consistent message. By telling

---

2. Ibid.

a joke with my hands while my face was a blank slate, or by telling a story of being physically exhausted as I stood erect, shoulders not slumping or sagging, I left my congregants feeling confused. Was I speaking sarcastically? Was there a touch of irony in the situation? The mixed messages the unintegrated, inconsistent parts of myself belied, signaled in this world of American Sign Language that something was not to be trusted, something was not to be taken at face value, or something essential was missing.

In my personal life, the demand to respond to *Ayekah?* with a whole-hearted *Hineni* became clear to me in a profound and life-transforming way when I was in my twenties. It was then that I recognized that I was neither what I was socialized to be nor what I had believed myself to be—that is, heterosexual. I had been socialized like all of my peers to be heterosexual. Yet in my teens I had a sense that many things I was doing were not honest expressions of what I was feeling. While my female friends were expressing genuine excitement and passion for their "romances," I wondered why I did not feel what they were feeling. However, I ignored the clear internal discomfort that gnawed at me, convinced that I was heterosexual.

Years later, I was able to understand that lack of harmony between my actions and my feelings: I was gay—not straight. I had been trying to force myself to be what I was not; there was no consistency between my external and internal selves. When I realized that I did not need to continue to live as I had, I was tremendously relieved, and incredibly frightened. Inside, this realization resonated as something radically different from my previous experience, something transformative. I began to feel more integrated than I ever had. Nevertheless, I was plagued by questions about my life plans and my future.

The exhilaration and terror I experienced when coming out to myself were heightened when I contemplated coming out to other people. Would people accept, understand, continue to value me, if they knew? The response of many of the significant people in my life to that simple question was hard for me to predict; so I did not risk it. However, in time, I came to suffer from the limitations imposed upon many of my existing relationships precisely because I did not feel able to share anything about my personal and emotional life. I realized that with people who did not know and with those whom I did not feel safe to tell, I shut down emotionally. I was able to take care of my professional and academic responsibilities, but I felt as if I were checking a part of myself at the door when I crossed the threshold into the social world. Eventually, I reached a point where I was unwilling to be only partially present. I was ready to say *Hineni* and to give people an opportunity to know me and accept me. It was then that I formulated a different question: How can I delude myself by thinking that people who do not know who I am, and who are ignorant about the people and relationships that make my life rich and full, are accepting *me?* It was then that I truly understood the rewards of taking the risk of being accepted or rejected as I am, as I was becoming.

We revel in the unbridled joy of a laughing or dancing

child because its whole being rejoices. We easily discern the difference between a performer whose technical skills are excellent but mechanical and a performer whose technical skills are complemented by a soul that expresses the whole being of the performer. So, too, we have the capacity to express our whole beings and to encourage others to do the same. To be present in the moment—to respond to the question *Ayekah?* with *Hineni*—is to bring one's whole self in its current state of becoming. To live in the moment, with a sense of connection to the past and the future, to let the self that we are express itself with integrity and wholeness, is to let our authentic selves be and become. To do this is terrifying and liberating at the same time. This double valence of saying "Here I am," complex yet integrated, is captured in the *Hineni* prayer. Called to a holy task, called to enter into relationship with God, is in fact the terror of our daily task of saying *Hineni*.

For Reform Jews, too, our goal is to say *Hineni* and to embrace our essential nature as *Ehyeh Asher Ehyeh*. As Reform Jews we recognize ourselves to be part of an evolving tradition. We affirm the existence of a tradition that is responsive to an ever-changing world. As we are ever in the process of becoming, individually and collectively, so our forms of expression are continually shifting and developing. Our people's liturgy, literature, communal structures, cultural and religious expressions have never been static. In our unique expression of Judaism we affirm the complex integrity of our people.

Shema—we have the capacity to hear the essential communication that takes place beyond the words. Israel—we are a complex yet unified entity, ever in the process of becoming. *Yisrael*—we each have the capacity to attend to the integrity we possess and to help others do the same. *Adonai Eloheinu*—our God, known as *Ehyeh Asher Ehyeh,* is an ever-changing entity whose form is constant. *Adonai Ehad*—our God's oneness is manifest through God's complexity and integrity. Created in God's likeness, we are called to express our godliness, our holiness, by affirming and expressing our own complexity and our own integrity, and to embrace ourselves and others in our ongoing process of becoming.